C000125477

ISBN: 978-1-9997787-1-2

First Edition

Find more at:

www.carlvernon.com

Other books by Carl Vernon

Anxiety Rebalance:
All the Answers You Need to Overcome Anxiety and
Depression

The Less-Stress Lifestyle:
Regain Control and Rediscover Happiness

Expect Change

HOW TO RECOGNISE AND DEAL WITH TOXIC BEHAVIOUR
AT WORK, AT HOME AND IN LIFE

Carl Vernon

Contents

Doing what is right for you

Before I released this book, I asked some of the people who are closest to me how best I should deliver the powerful message you'll find in these pages. I also asked my social media and community followers to tell me about any toxic behaviour they had experienced, and I was inundated with stories! I heard about everything from toxic parents to toxic bosses (some of their stories you'll read in this book). As a result of the advice I got and the stories I heard, I decided to put this chapter at the beginning of the book.

I hoped this book would help countless people change their lives for the better, but I also knew that dealing with toxic behaviour would have knock-on effects on children, jobs and lifestyles. I want to help people grow and change their lives, but I don't want to put them in a situation they find difficult to cope with.

Some people told me they thought you should deal with toxic behaviour – you only have one life, and it's way too short to put up with people who are no good for you. On the other hand, I also heard about people who had tried to deal with toxic behaviour in their life, and had ended up putting themselves in a worse situation.

My conclusion is: dealing with toxic behaviour in your life is *never* easy. If your partner is toxic, this will have a negative effect on your children. Sometimes we need to think of others before ourselves. Perhaps a friend you've known for many years is guilty of toxic behaviour, and losing their friendship would leave a big gap in your life. It could be a family member you love but don't like very much, and the decision between loyalty and happiness is tearing you apart. If your boss is toxic, dealing with him could mean big changes in your job, career and lifestyle. Whatever the situation, dealing with toxic behaviour *will* change your life. This process will be challenging, especially at first, but it will be worth it.

I wrote this book to make the subject of toxic behaviour more accessible. We don't speak about it enough. If we do, it's usually in a negative way – through gossip or behind somebody's back, instead of talking to the toxic person directly.

Toxic behaviour is something many of us accept as part of our lives, and we rarely do anything about it. But with education and awareness, people can change. If we can communicate more about how we feel, both to the people in our lives and to ourselves, we can vastly improve our lives.

I wanted to achieve the same thing with my first book, *Anxiety Rebalance*. I wanted to take a difficult subject – anxiety – and make it more accessible, and make it easier for people to talk about it. Based on feedback from readers, I think I have achieved my goal.

I know I'm tackling a big subject in this book, and there might be many reasons why you've been putting up with toxic behaviour. These reasons might have a lot to do with the potential effects on children, the loss of a job, ending a relationship, or a significant lifestyle change. Before you read on, if you have any doubts about your situation, including whether or not you should try to change it, think about whether or not moving on is the best solution for you.

If you fear that dealing with toxic behaviour in your life might put you in a worse situation, the timing may not be right. For example, if you face up to a toxic boss and that means you risk losing a job you can't afford to lose, keeping a roof over your head is more important at this point. That's no problem. Pick up the book again at a later date, when you feel the timing is right.

How do you know when the timing is right?

Only you can answer this question. When it comes to doing the hard things in life, including dealing with toxic behaviour, you could argue that the timing is *never* right.

The timing is right when you know you're in a good place mentally. By 'a good place', I mean a stable and well-grounded place, where your decisions are well thought out and rational: a place where you feel unafraid, strong and ready to face the challenges that come with making difficult decisions.

Fear might be one of the reasons you're dealing with toxic behaviour right now. Toxic people depend on fear to keep you in your place. Fear will naturally come with change, but if you don't make the decision to deal with fear, you might find that nothing in your life changes.

What I'm asking you to do, before you proceed, is to use your common sense. There is an obvious reason why you've picked up this book. I want you to understand the changes that will take place in your life when you start implementing what I'm going to show you. If you're not ready for these changes, and you don't feel like you're in a strong enough place yet, work on that first.

It all starts with a change in mindset (the way you think about things, including your attitude towards someone or something), so begin there. Start mentally adjusting yourself to the fact that you want change, and therefore change is coming. When you do that, you expect change, and you'll deal with it in a more positive way. You'll embrace it and want it.

When you've reached this point, read on, because you have an exciting journey ahead of you.

A personal journey of change

Not long ago, I'd have been too embarrassed to admit that I was a weak person. I'd much rather mask my insecurities and deep unhappiness with pretence and a fake smile. The fact that I'm able to write about my weakness in this book proves to me how much stronger I've become.

The biggest part of my transition from weakness was, without doubt, changing my relationship with other people – including being able to recognise and deal with toxic behaviour.

I've realised that lots of people in my life have been bad for me. Some of the people closest to me have pushed me beyond what should be acceptable. Foster parents have treated me with contempt. Work colleagues have prioritised their bonuses and promotion opportunities over loyalty. Teachers have told me I would never amount to anything. Friends have used information I told them in confidence to destroy other relationships. Toxic bosses have made my working life hell. I've had the lot.

As a grown man, I've sat in my car and sobbed uncontrollably, wondering how anybody could treat me or another human being so badly. I've sat up in the middle of the night, unable to sleep, watching motivational videos on YouTube, hoping they would give me the courage to get through the next day. I've played loud music, in the hope it would drown out my anxiety-driven and fearful thoughts.

One of my earliest memories is from when I was five. I came downstairs one morning, to see my mother had two big black eyes. I asked her what had happened. As she quickly tried to cover her eyes with sunglasses, she replied, 'Oh, I walked into the door.' The reality was, after a heavy drinking session, my alcoholic father had punched her so hard in the face he'd given her two huge black eyes. She could barely see.

I could give more examples, but I'll sum up by saying I was homeless for a while as a kid, I've been in foster care, and I've had many challenges to overcome in my life. For me, however, the saddest thing is knowing that, even though I can give you many examples of hardship, lots of you will have had it tougher than I have. And I don't need to search far for such stories. My partner of fifteen years has many stories of her own to tell, including about her alcoholic parents, who used to keep her up every night throughout her childhood, screaming at and physically abusing each other.

But here's the deal: each of my experiences has made me a better person. It would have been very easy to go down the route of hurting other people and being toxic myself. I could have continued the same dysfunctional behaviour that was, in my environment, normal, and continued the destructive cycle that toxic behaviour creates. But I chose a different route, and a lot of that has to do with the fact that there are genuinely good people out there. When you read on, I don't want you to forget this important fact.

As well as toxic people, there are some astonishingly kind, caring and loving human beings out there. Some of them risk their own lives so you can live a free life. Some travel across the globe to help starving children. Some help starving people in their own country to get fed, stay clothed, and have a place to sleep at night.

With this book, my intention is *not* to judge others. I am far from perfect. I don't always get it right, and I, like everyone else, make mistakes. I want this book to be used as a tool for good. I want it to empower people who are being abused to take action. I want it to stop the cycle of toxic behaviour. I want it to help you wake up and smell the coffee, so you realise that you deserve more from life, and understand that life has more to offer than abuse, bullying, ridicule, negativity and hate.

I'm no idealist. I don't believe we can live in a utopia where we all skip and frolic through the fields without a care in the world. However, I do believe we were all born good, and through experiences and many other factors, some people turn bad. We'll discuss why this happens a little – but we won't dwell on it too much. Our focus, time and energy are better spent on solutions, so we can concentrate on making our life richer and freer, rather than on wondering why toxic people do what they do.

I've managed to improve my life by dealing with the toxicity in it – I didn't allow the past to dictate my future. This journey was far from plain sailing. On many occasions I gave people too many chances – and sometimes I paid for it. You'll find many of the lessons I learned in this book.

When I made the changes I'm about to show you in this book, my happiness and well-being began to improve. I have no doubt that reading this book will improve your life too.

Toxicity is real

There are lots of things in life that are obviously dangerous, and so we know to avoid them. Toxic people aren't always obvious, but the damage they cause is clear.

Heart disease, heart attacks, strokes, cancer and other life-threatening illnesses are all linked to too much stress. And what is one of the leading causes of stress? You got it – toxic people. A toxic boss alone is enough to put you in hospital. If toxicity is not dealt with, it will have serious consequences for your health.

How you feel on the inside is intrinsically linked to your health. I spent years dealing with constant illnesses due to too much stress. A big part of that was having too much toxicity in my life. Since I've detoxified my life, I'm much happier for it. My well-being has been given a huge boost, and illnesses are a thing of the past. I have no doubt that if I'd continued to allow toxicity to spread in my life, it would only be a matter of time before it caused a serious illness.

It would be nice if toxic people were made to wear a 'toxic' sign so you could avoid them. (Maybe a big yellow sticker with a skull on it, stuck to their head?) That's probably never going to happen, so to protect yourself against their sometimes invisible toxicity, you have to hone your toxic-identifying skills. Like a sniffer dog at an airport, you have to be able to sniff them out.

Toxicity may sometimes be invisible, but I've seen people battered and bruised by it. I've seen people in abusive relationships. I've seen people become seriously ill because of the actions of a toxic person. I've met people who have had to take time off work because of a toxic boss or colleague. I've met people whose lives have been destroyed by a toxic friend. I've met people who have toxic parents who have manipulated and controlled them their entire lives.

I've met parents who are at their wits' end because of their child's behaviour. Just the other day, I read an article in a newspaper about a young girl who had committed suicide by hanging herself in her school toilets because she couldn't take being bullied any longer. She was only sixteen, and had her whole life ahead of her.

I don't need to see statistics about abuse and bullying to know how common it is. If I've personally seen all these things, then you probably also have – or experienced them yourself.

Toxicity is real, and its effects should never be underestimated. Picking up this book gives you a big advantage: it will help you to understand toxicity better, and also tell you how to effectively deal with it.

The journey

Come on a journey with me. On this journey, feel free to laugh, cry, or shout at the sky as you embrace your new discoveries and freedom. Feel the toxicity drain away as you decide to serve notice on people you realise are no good for you. Learn how to develop stronger and better relationships with the people who deserve to be in your life. Arm yourself with the determination that, from this moment forward, you will no longer put up with anything or anyone you deem toxic. Most exciting of all, *expect change*.

If at times I sound a little harsh and direct, it's only because I want to emphasise to you how important it is that you listen to what I have to say. I care for you and your well-being, and I know how detrimental it can be to have toxicity in your life. Toxic people tend to follow the same habits, behaviours and patterns. Over the years, these behaviours have become more obvious to me, and you'll soon recognise them for yourself.

I've split the book into three parts. Part 1 will help you to recognise toxic people and their traits. Part 2 will help you discover yourself by recognising your own habits and behaviours, including how they might be encouraging a toxic influence. Part 3 will give you the tools and knowledge you need to deal with toxic people so you can start detoxifying your life, allowing you to move forward in a new direction.

If you're ready to expect change, let's start by looking at toxic traits.

PART 1: RECOGNISING TOXIC BEHAVIOUR AND ITS NEGATIVE EFFECTS

Toxic traits

I like the word 'toxic'. I think it sums up certain people and their behaviour very well. If you think about how toxicity works, it's very similar to how the wrong people in your life act towards you. The most obvious is the negative effect their behaviour has on you, and how easily and quickly the toxicity can spread.

Throughout this book, when I refer to 'toxic', 'toxic people', 'toxicity' or the 'wrong people', I will be referring to all the people who have a negative effect on your life. In this instance, it means anybody who is bullying, abusing, harassing, intimidating, controlling or manipulating you.

A toxic person could be somebody very close to you – a parent, partner, boss, friend, sibling, colleague, teacher, anybody – and they come in all shapes and sizes. The odds are, you have toxic people in your life right now. I know this because everybody has. Toxic people affect us all, and nobody is immune.

Some are easy to recognise because their toxicity oozes out of them through their words and actions. Some are a little less obvious, which is why it's important to know and recognise their traits.

Being able to recognise toxic people will seriously transform your life, because as soon as you start to deal with the toxicity, it will feel as though a huge weight has been lifted off your shoulders. You'll no longer have to wear a mask and pretend to be somebody you're not. You'll feel like a new person, with a new sense of freedom, passion and purpose.

Allowing toxicity in your life is dangerous. If a factory producing chocolate bars discovered that one of the ingredients it was using was toxic, would it continue production? Of course not. The factory would be shut down so that the problem could be dealt with before it spread and got worse. If the factory sent the chocolate bars out for sale, they would make people ill. The problem would spread, and eventually it would shut the entire business down. In this instance, the chocolate factory is your life, and the toxic ingredient is the toxic people in your life. How long are you going to allow the toxicity to permeate your life before you start to deal with it?

But let's be fair. Nobody is perfect; we all have bad days, right? We all like a gossip and have a bit of toxicity in us. Confusing toxic behaviour with normal, everyday behaviour can lead to you cutting *everybody* out of your life, which is why I want to define what I mean by a toxic person here.

Toxic people always have drama in their life
A toxic person survives on drama. They aren't
satisfied unless they are duelling with at least three
people at a time. They are addicted to drama; it's
almost as though they can't survive without it. Drama
is never far away from a toxic person. Nothing brings
toxic people together more than something that isn't
their business. If there is a small chance that they can
create drama, a toxic person will take it.

Toxic people rarely have anything good to say
You won't find a toxic person saying nice things
about other people. In fact, you won't get much
positivity at all from them – apart from when it's
about them. It's rare that a toxic person will ask you
how you are or how your day has been, because they
don't care about you. They're only concerned about
their day and how they are. Everything else is
insignificant to them. When you get into a
conversation with a toxic person, it will be focused on
negativity. No matter how positive something is, they
will find something negative to say about it.

**Toxic people are quick to criticise and judge
others**
Due to their own judgemental mentality, toxic people
believe their own lives are perfect, and nobody else
can get close to that perfection. Toxic people have a
tendency to speak before they think and often offend
others. Where you might think something, and keep it

to yourself because you know you risk offending, a toxic person will just voice their thought without regard for the person's feelings. In conversation, a toxic person will stand out because their conversation will be based on how much they dislike somebody because of their weight, looks, personality, race, creed or anything else they can judge. All these things are easy targets, and allow the toxic person to vent their anger on something and someone who is different to them. Differences can be intimidating and, rather than make an effort to understand a person who is different, a toxic person will act aggressively towards them.

Toxic people are passive-aggressive
As well as being directly aggressive, toxic people are also passive-aggressive. This is a common trait for many toxic people. If a toxic person gives you a compliment, it will usually be back-handed. If he tells you that you look beautiful, he'll back it up by saying, 'But your arse looks big.' Toxic people are also good at denying their passive-aggressive nature by saying 'I'm only joking – can't you take a joke?' They'll use this when making a back-handed comment, or saying something really offensive. They're not joking – they mean every word – but trying to mask comments as jokes means they can say offensive things more often. Sometimes the passive-aggressive behaviour is hidden. For example, a work colleague might intentionally sabotage your project by making a mistake, making it look as though you are incompetent. A lot of toxic people aren't ashamed to

hide their passive-aggressive nature. In this case, they'll make remarks that they know will offend you, but will deliver them in a way that is – on the surface – normal and acceptable. Ignoring and sulking are also common passive-aggressive behaviours. You can rest assured, a passive-aggressive toxic person will always have to have the last word.

Toxic people are jealous
If a toxic person sees somebody driving a car they admired, they're much more likely to sneer at the driver than look in admiration. They won't appreciate that the person driving the car might have worked hard to afford it; instead, they will think that the person must have in some way been given an advantage, and therefore don't deserve to be driving the car. A toxic person is likely to accuse their partner of cheating on them, even if they have no evidence of this. This is partly to do with their own insecurities, and the fact that they hate to feel as though they might be cheated or tricked. It could also be that they are cheating themselves. It's a similar story when working towards a goal. Rather than focus on getting it done, they will give every excuse for why it won't, and didn't, work. Even if they put little effort into making it work, if it failed, it's because they were in some way cheated.

Toxic people have a 'who cares, anyway?' mentality

A toxic person says things like 'What does it matter anyway? We're all going to die', and 'There's going to be a civil war soon anyway'. This gives them a 'nothing to lose' mentality. You should always be wary of somebody who believes they haven't got anything to lose.

Toxic people are manipulative
Because of their direct manner and strong negative views, toxic people are usually manipulative. They like to get everybody else on board with their views, and will target vulnerable people who are easier to manipulate. You'll find the most charismatic toxic people leading groups that spread hate and violence. Other toxic people will be keen to follow.

Toxic people lie a lot and exaggerate the truth
Toxic people get wrapped up in their own lies. To save face, they will often see their lies as the truth. These lies can sometimes be embarrassingly bizarre and completely unfounded, but a toxic person will look you right in the eye and convince you they're telling the truth. Some professionals say this is because they believe their lies to be true. I don't know about that. What I do know is that it's very difficult to have a relationship with somebody who consistently lies.

Toxic people have to win

Most people are competitive. There is nothing wrong with healthy competition – it's what drives people to achieve. But winning isn't enough for a toxic person. For them, everybody else has to lose. They have to see everybody else fail. Playing fair isn't in their vocabulary, and they'll do whatever it takes to make sure they crush their opposition. You often see this type of behaviour in business, but the mentality can permeate other areas of their lives. If they have this attitude in business, for example, it's likely they will have it towards their family. They'll teach the same mentality to their children, turning a relaxed game of football into the most important match since the last World Cup final.

Toxic people rarely, if ever, apologise
Apologising would mean a toxic person admitting they are wrong, and because they believe they're never wrong, they never apologise. It takes a big person to admit when they're wrong, and toxic people aren't big people. A toxic person is more likely to defend their actions than apologise for them. They will always be able to justify how they have acted, and they will expect you to quickly forgive them. For example, if a toxic friend uses information against you, they'll say they did it for your benefit, and you should forgive them because you've been friends for years. This is also common for toxic parents – you should forgive and forget because 'I'm your parent'. An apology is seen as a major weakness, so don't expect one anytime soon, no matter how heinous the act.

Toxic people don't see the wrong in what they do

Toxic people rarely blame themselves for anything. If they do something wrong, their behaviour is always justified, no matter how horrible it is. *I hit you because I love you so much.* You'll find it incredibly difficult to show or prove to a toxic person that their behaviour isn't appropriate or right.

Toxic people act as judge and jury

There is no grey area for a toxic person. Everything is either black or white. You're either in their good books, or you are their enemy. Something as small as you not sharing their views or opinions is enough to banish you. If they believe you are working against them, it is impossible to convince them of anything else. They will act as judge and jury, and no amount of reasonable doubt will be good enough. The judgement will be harsh, snappy and unfair. A life sentence for a petty misdemeanour is common.

Toxic people play the victim

Just as they don't see the wrong in what they do, toxic people will not claim ownership of, or responsibility for, a situation or problem. The fact that they 'didn't ask to be born' gives them the right to be unsympathetic towards others. They will quickly pass the buck, and will often say 'it's not my fault'. Being a martyr means that all their misfortunes and failings are someone else's fault. They believe that playing the victim lets them off the hook, which makes it much easier for them to justify their dismissive and unforgiving mentality and behaviour towards others. Why should they change? If anything, it's you who should change, not them.

Toxic people care about what people think
Even though toxic people don't particularly like people, they care about what people think. They will say things like 'You humiliated me'. Toxic people are usually insecure and paranoid, and will overanalyse what people say. They will easily take offence and believe something to be an insult when it's not. They don't like to think the wool is being pulled over their eyes, and if they think they are being tricked or cheated, they will quickly become angry and potentially violent.

Toxic people make you feel like you need to prove yourself
One of the most annoying traits of a toxic person is how they believe everybody should prove themselves to them. A toxic friend might make you feel as though your life is insignificant compared to theirs, and that you have a long way to go to get close to their perfection. This is part of their manipulative behaviour: they'll get you trying to prove your loyalty towards them. They could be physically and/or mentally abusing you, and will still expect you to show them your undying gratitude and respect. They think you should be grateful that they've chosen you to be in their lives, no matter how they treat you. A toxic parent or sibling might regularly remind you

that 'blood is thicker than water', and going against what they say or their actions is betraying their loyalty.

Toxic people intentionally look to destroy

If a toxic person doesn't agree with something, such as a relationship or friendship, they will go all out to destroy it. They will lie, bad-mouth, stir up information, and do anything they feel is necessary to achieve their destruction. They might feel as though they are protecting you, but they are more concerned about achieving what they believe to be right, no matter the consequences or how much it might hurt you. It's common for a toxic person to constantly fall out with neighbours and regularly argue with them. If they live in a place long enough, they will find reasons to hate people within the vicinity of their home.

Toxic people hold grudges

Because they have an unforgiving mentality, toxic people hold grudges. They may hold a grudge for years, sometimes decades, and they feel as strongly about it years later as they do when it began. They might mention it in an argument or disagreement when you least expect them to, and it might be used as the basis of all future confrontations. They find it difficult to forgive and let things go because toxic people are governed by pride. It's likely they will seek to revenge the grudge in some form, usually with a petty act like signing you up to spam. The need for revenge is due to their insecurity and inadequacy, and the fact they can't cope with the thought that somebody might have beaten them or got one up on them.

Toxic people show up when they're least expected

Just as when animals go into hibernation, a toxic person can disappear for a long time and suddenly come back into your life without warning. They typically come out of hibernation when someone close to them dies, or a friend/family member has had some success or good luck – such as winning money. Toxic people enjoy keeping their neighbours awake throughout the night with music and loud parties, and there is no better time to do it than when the sun is out. If somebody dies, a toxic person will be quick to find out if they are due any inheritance. They'll ask questions about the person's possessions, and make a claim to anything that takes their fancy, showing little remorse for the person who has died. If someone connected to a toxic person becomes successful, usually in relation to money or fame, a toxic person will look to make contact and establish a relationship with that person, even if they haven't seen them for decades. Just as when a death occurs, they will try to stake a claim on the fame and fortune, and expect a cut. It's not unusual for a toxic person to regularly ask a friend or family for money, if they believe their friend or family member has money to give. They will in some way believe that because they are your friend or connected to you as a family member, they are entitled to your money. Another reason why a toxic person might show up in your life after a while is because their current lackey(s) have wised up and told them to do one. Rather than go out looking for a new one, they'll try to rekindle old relationships with people they have taken advantage of previously. Toxic people are always quick to drop relationships if they believe something/someone better is on the horizon. (By 'better', I mean someone who will fulfil their needs more.)

Toxic people use privately shared information against you

Unless you want your private life bandied around or used against you, don't share it with a toxic person. You can be at your lowest point, reaching out for a helping hand, and whatever information you share at that moment, you can guarantee it will come up again. It might not be that day, or even that month, but a toxic person will bank the information and use it against you at a later date. It might be used in an argument, to blackmail you or to intimidate you. Have you noticed how many politicians are involved in scandals? They all relate to secrets that have escaped into the public domain. Imagine the information being used as blackmail for getting things done. (If you have any doubt about this, I suggest you watch the TV series *House of Cards*. It's not only brilliant, but it's also a fabulous insight into toxic behaviour!)

Toxic people are unpredictable

Toxic people struggle to control their anger and emotions, and have regular outbursts of rage. Their behaviour can be confusing: they might treat some people very well, and others with absolute contempt. For example, Bob might appear to be the friendliest person at work, but when he goes home he beats his wife. They appear incapable of controlling themselves around the people who accept their behaviour (their victims). If they have an outburst, they are usually apologetic afterwards, but it doesn't stop them from doing it again.

Toxic people are narcissistic and delusional

Toxic people have a way of making everything about them. If you speak to them about a problem you have, they have an amazing knack of turning the conversation back to themselves. If you say your cat died, then they'll tell you two of their cats died last week. Also, try telling a toxic person about one of your achievements. They'll either need to walk away, or top it. So if you're competing in the high jump at the next Olympics, a toxic person used to be a champion high jumper until they got an ankle injury and had to quit the sport. If he were still a high jumper, he believes he would be better than you. He simply can't deal with the fact that somebody might be better than him at anything. The jealousy will ooze out of his words and body like ... you guessed it ... toxic fluid.

Toxic people have few friends

Toxic people prefer to have few friends (if any) because it means fewer people to control. They don't like to make personal connections because they believe friendship isn't worth the hassle. Positive personal connections are a sign of weakness, not joy. They believe that all relationships will turn sour, so they'll protect themselves. It's common for toxic people to be reclusive, spending lots of time on their own, because they prefer their own company to that of others. They will rarely, if ever, go to social events. If they do go, it may be a nightmare: by the end of the event, they would have picked at least one fight or said something highly inappropriate to somebody. If they do have friends, they are more likely to see them as pawns, constantly reviewing what they can get from the relationship. Because they see you as either a friend or an enemy, toxic people are quick to cut people out of their life. Also, since only a few people are willing to put up with their toxic behaviour, it doesn't leave many people in their circle.

Toxic people will bring you down to their level

Toxic people are deeply unhappy (but most of the time they like to pretend this is far from the truth). This poses the question: Why do people become toxic? As I mentioned in the Introduction, we'll continue to focus on finding solutions to toxic behaviour rather than wondering why it happens.

Toxic people take pleasure in making people feel bad, and will try to bring others down with them. *If I'm unhappy, why should you be happy?* Toxic people don't appreciate that it takes more effort to stay positive; rather than make that effort, they will try to bring people down.

Sinking ships

Toxic people have lots of other characteristics and behaviours. It's the last point in the above list that is the most important because toxic people will bring you down without remorse or hesitation. Toxicity can be so powerful that it can drag the nicest people into its clutches, sometimes without them seeing it coming.

Identifying the toxic behaviour in your life, and doing something about it, will prevent you from lots of unnecessary hardship and unhappiness. Why? Because toxic people are like sinking ships. Their lives are a mess, and they have absolutely no problem with taking everybody else down with them. In fact, it's exactly what they want. *If I'm unhappy and miserable, then so should you be.*

Don't take it personally. It rarely has anything to do with a specific person. It's more to do with the fact that toxic people thrive on drama – so they make it their job to create drama – in all areas of life. That's why you'll find toxic behaviour in all walks of life: at work, at home, at school, everywhere – even when you go on holiday. Drama is always waiting around the corner, and if you're in the vicinity, you'll be swept along with it.

It makes sense: toxic people tend to associate with other toxic people, and this increases the chances of drama. If it isn't them directly causing the drama, somebody else in their life is, so it's still going to have an effect. If you're the one closest to them (because you are one of the few people tolerating them and their behaviour), you'll bear the brunt of their dysfunctional behaviour. The longer you put up with it, the worse it gets, until you become their full-time lackey.

The way a toxic person hurts others isn't always obvious, as it is with verbal and physical abuse. It could be something like not taking the time to play with or care for their child, preferring instead to go to the pub. They might prioritise buying booze or fags over buying food for their family. These are some of the worst forms of toxic behaviour because if you're a kid, you're totally dependent on your parent/guardian to provide for you. If they don't, that's a form of abuse. If there is plenty of food in the cupboards but the child is starved of love and affection, that's also abusive.

Separating the behaviour from the person
There is a reason why the subtitle of this book says 'toxic behaviour' and not 'toxic people'. Sometimes you have to separate the behaviour from the person.

Recently I shared a post on my social media that said: 'Everybody you meet is fighting a battle you know nothing about. Be kind. Always.' This post was popular for a reason: it's entirely accurate. We are all fighting a battle – some of us are fighting big ones, daily. This can mean we all end up demonstrating toxic behaviour.

Some people don't realise how toxic they are. It's common for toxic people to have been hurt in the past (most likely in their childhood) and, because *they* were hurt, they want to hurt others. It takes a big person to be hurt and to continue to love and care for other people, which is why toxic behaviour is common. The dysfunctional behaviour goes around and around in a cycle until somebody decides to change the pattern.

In some circumstances, a little sympathy and understanding is necessary. But I want to make one thing absolutely clear: toxic people will *always* cause you hardship, however forgiving or accepting you choose to be.

As you read this book you'll discover why this is true – and also how to protect yourself against it.

We can all demonstrate toxic traits. Does that mean we're all toxic?

As I mentioned, we can all be a little toxic. You probably read the list above and recognised some behaviours that you do. If you did, don't worry. At some point we've all demonstrated toxic behaviour. We've all had a gossip or bad-mouthed somebody behind their back. Affairs and one-night stands are commonplace. In business, we're expected to be ruthless or face the prospect of being beaten by our competition, which can create its own toxic behaviour. It's all part of human nature.

However, there are two key ingredients that stand out. These two things are *consistency* and *intent*.

It's the people who *consistently* demonstrate the traits I covered above, with *intent* to do harm, who you should be wary of – the people who behave in that way on a regular enough basis that their behaviour affects others. These are the toxic people you need to watch out for and do something about. These people will do considerable damage to your health, well-being and welfare.

Humans can be unpredictable. A good egg can turn bad. (And vice versa, although a bad egg is a lot less likely to turn good.) If a person has proven himself to be trustworthy, then it's likely he will continue to be trustworthy. It's in his nature to be trustworthy and at the very core of who he is. If he's demonstrated he can be deceitful then, following the same principle, he's likely to continue to be deceitful. You judge someone based on their previous behaviour – because that's all you can do.

It's impossible to predict the future, just as it's impossible for us to know who is going to be wrong for us and who isn't. Unless their behaviour is obvious, giving you an opportunity to avoid it, we're going to slip up and perhaps sometimes we'll trust someone who turns out not to deserve our trust. As well as equipping yourself with the knowledge you'll gain from this book, you need to use your common sense and instinct – two important tools to carry with you on your journey.

The best way to do this is to act like Spider-Man and use your Spider-Sense (instinct). You'll know when something doesn't feel quite right.

Your instincts are very powerful, so don't disregard them. Your instincts are the gut feelings you get about something. Does it *feel* right? Or does it make you feel uneasy? If something doesn't feel right, keep your distance while you do some more digging. When it comes to toxicity, you're always best to err on the side of caution and scepticism. Jumping into any type of relationship with a toxic person, whether personal or business-related, is risky. Instead, take your time and be patient.

Judge people by their actions

What people say and what people do are two very different things. I've come to realise that it's what people *do* that is really important. Talk is cheap.

If you are in any doubt about whether or not somebody in your life is wrong for you, always judge them on their actions. If she tells you she's going to meet you at seven o'clock, but she shows up nonchalantly at eight without any apology, that action should speak louder than words about who she is – especially if she's often late (and unapologetic). Through her action, she's basically saying she doesn't care about inconveniencing you.

If you're in a relationship and he doesn't act in a loving way towards you, there's a strong chance he doesn't love you. Naturally, a ten-year relationship won't have the same spark and intense passion as a relationship in its honeymoon period, but he should still show you he loves you. Romantic gestures (giving you a hug, taking you out for a meal or buying you flowers, for example) might be rare, but by doing them he's still showing you he loves you. It's when they completely dry up that you need to start paying attention.

Actions speak louder than words, so you need to start paying attention to them. Words are easy to say, but actions never lie.

No matter what he tells you, always judge him on his past behaviour. What he's done in the past, he'll continue to do.

If your partner has cheated on his last three girlfriends but promises he'll never cheat on you, I hate to break it to you, but the odds say he will cheat – if he hasn't already. Compare your unfaithful partner to a man who has been married for ten years, and split up with his wife because she was unfaithful to him. You might find the difference in their characters to be gulfs apart. Does this guarantee the latter man will be the ideal partner, who will show you the respect you deserve? Of course not. But somebody's past behaviour is the best predictor of their future behaviour.

If the guy you interviewed last week promised he'd be your next top performer, but all he's done in his career is demonstrate a lack of drive, passion or ambition, including lots of job-hopping, it's highly likely he'll be a waste of your time. Compare him to a guy who is already a top performer who you had to headhunt because he was busy being a top performer. The latter man has already proved himself.

Judging people in this way might sound harsh, especially considering how people can change. But what else can you do? A person's history is *the* strongest gauge of their future.

I look at everything – from the way they live their lives to the people they have in their lives. Why? Because that will tell me everything I need to know. I know that their actions will always speak louder than their words.

How many chances should you give someone?

When someone is behaving badly to you, how many chances do you give somebody? Only you can answer that. In my experience, giving someone too many chances leads to you being taken advantage of. It's the classic 'give an inch and they take a mile' scenario.

Kids do this all the time – it's how they learn how to behave. When they grab a chair to climb up to the biscuit cupboard, they'll wait for their parents to say 'stop'. Until that point, they'll keep climbing and pushing the boundaries. If 'stop' never comes, they'll feast on biscuits for breakfast, before dinner, and before they go to bed (at whatever time they choose to go). That makes them believe they can not only help themselves to biscuits whenever they want, but that they can do what they like, when they like.

Biscuit hunting isn't the crime of the century, but if they aren't told to stop, what will they try next? And after that? Like a snowball effect, their behaviour will keep getting worse if they're not told to stop in a firm, clear way that is effective.

If you've ever come across an unruly kid with no boundaries, you'll know how important it is to set clear boundaries for children early. You need to do the same thing with toxic people because, like kids, they'll keep pushing until they hear 'stop'. It's up to the person setting the boundaries to stay firm.

We need to decide what we will allow to happen to us, and this will depend on our standards, including what we expect and how we allow others to treat us. (We'll cover standards in more detail in Part 2.)

Can people change?

There is a very strong argument to suggest that people can change, but also an equally strong argument to say they can't. I'll discuss both sides of the debate in this book.

Experience has shown me that, if somebody *really* wants to change, they will. If they don't, they won't. There are lots of contributory factors behind this, and if you're in their life, you'll be one of them. If you're not enough of a reason for them to want to change, there isn't anything you can do about it.

Usually, people deserve the chance to redeem themselves or explain their behaviour. There is always a reason why people do things, and sometimes it's fair to separate the person from the behaviour. I believe that most people do want to change for the better, but they just don't know *how* to do it.

People change because of education and awareness. Being aware of negative aspects of your behaviour means you can change. Being unaware of your behaviour means you might not believe you have anything to change. A good question to ask is: How aware of their behaviour is this person? If they're completely unaware of their actions and the ramifications of those actions, there's very little you can do about it.

People are sexist, ageist, racist (and all the other -ists) due to ignorance. Dealing with someone who might be different to them takes them out of their comfort zone and, rather than get educated, they choose the easier route and deal with it by using hate.

Some people are completely unaware of the effects of their actions and behaviour on others. With a bit of education, they can change their behaviour and attitudes. When I think back to some of the things I did when I was younger, I cringe. I changed my behaviour thanks to education. I re-educated myself so well, I completely changed my outlook on life. So I suppose I'm saying that I changed and, if I changed, others can too.

Some people, due to their environment or other circumstances, haven't been given the opportunity to get educated and become aware. If they are told about their actions, they may be sufficiently motivated to make significant changes. (We'll cover this more in Part 3.)

Some people simply don't want to change. They want to stay ignorant, and don't care about their actions. It's up to you to gauge who you're dealing with. If you're dealing with somebody who doesn't want to change by getting educated and becoming aware, how are you going to get them to change? Let's put it this way: if you have a friend you've known for a long time, and she has never made an effort to call you or arrange to meet you – and you realise you always instigate getting together – stop calling them. You'll soon find out if your friendship is worth anything if you receive a call or message. If your friend continues to be selfish and disregard your feelings, you won't get a call. If so, were they really a friend?

Some of the people closest to me have been through tremendous personal change. They have gone from desperate situations to become some of the nicest and kindest people you could wish to meet. They did it by taking the opportunity to become educated and aware. This changed their lives. That proved to me that, yes, people *can* change. But I've also been in situations where I've thought somebody has changed, only for them to show that they haven't.

Apart from judging somebody on their previous actions, here are some questions to ask yourself if you're considering ending your relationship with them.

Can you forgive them for what they've done? If you can't, it's likely you'll end up demonstrating toxic behaviour yourself. If you can't leave the past where it is, there is no moving forward.

Are you sad when you're not with them? Ending a relationship will leave a hole in anybody's life, but is your life worse when they're not around? Or are you just with them because you're lonely?

Does it hurt your pride to think you have to make the first move? Are you fed up having to be the one who always makes the first move? Do you always have to be the first to apologise? Pride has no place in a decent relationship, and feeling this way is a strong indication that the relationship isn't right.

Are you less or more effective without them? How stressed do they make you feel? Do they make you feel insecure, guilty or unloved? Or do you lack motivation and get-up-and-go when they're not around? If you do, maybe they were better for you than you thought.

Some people genuinely need help to resolve issues. Addictions, abuse, uncontrolled anger – all these things require help from a professional. If you love the person involved, and you want the best for them, you should do your best to make sure they get the help they need. But if they show no interest in wanting help, or they've tried to get help on numerous previous occasions and nothing has changed, what can you do? You can lead a horse to water, but you can't make him drink.

Offering endless chances to somebody who doesn't want to change will only be at the expense of your own well-being.

Stick to your ultimatums
If you decide to keep giving chances, they will usually come with ultimatums. If they do, you need to stick to them. If you don't, you'll be seen as weak – weaker than before – and you might find that the behaviour gets worse. The more you fail to stick to ultimatums, generally, the worse the behaviour gets. Through your lack of action, you're telling your partner/friend/boss/kid that they can do what they like – and they'll continue to get away with it. If your kid keeps climbing up to reach the biscuit tin, and you keep telling them to stop without enforcing any ultimatum, they will keep on climbing.

Your common sense should tell you if the person deserves a chance, or more than one chance. This will depend on the person, their actions, how well you know them, and how much you love them. You then have to be strong – to make sure you go through with what you have decided to do.

Consider other people's thoughts, feelings and needs – but not to the detriment of your health and well-being. There is a reason why airlines tell you to put an oxygen mask on yourself before you put one on your kids. If *you* can't breathe, how are you going to help your children breathe? You can't give something you haven't got.

The Negative Effect

I know that life isn't always black and white, but I also know that life is short. We don't have time to waste on people who will drag us down and make us miserable. Sometimes we have to be a little ruthless if we want a glimpse of the rainbow. And that means being able to suss out toxic people.

An effective technique to do this is what I call *The Negative Effect*. This is very simple, and here's how it works.

STEP 1:
Pick a person in your life. It can be anybody. If you have a suspicion that someone might be toxic, pick them.

STEP 2:
Grab a pen and paper, and draw a line down the middle of the sheet of paper. On one side, at the top of the left column write POSITIVE, and on the top of the right column, write NEGATIVE.

STEP 3:
Think about the last conversation you had with this person. (This step requires you to have a good memory, so if you don't, you'll have to start the exercise after you next meet the person you've picked.)

As you go through your conversation, put a tick in the POSITIVE column for every positive thing that was said, and a tick in the NEGATIVE column for every negative thing that was said.

The positive things you talk about should be obvious. The most obvious negatives are things that relate to gossip and criticising others.

To be extra fair, put a tick in the positive box for anything you both discussed that was neutral – something you wouldn't consider positive or negative.

If you want to make this step super-easy, just score the entire conversation as positive or negative.

STEP 4:
Don't forget to have fun with this. Life is serious enough.

STEP 5:

Now go back as far as you can remember, and
continue to rate as many conversations and
interactions as you can with this person.

In this step, it will be much easier for you to take the
super-easy option of simply scoring each interaction
as positive or negative.

STEP 6:
Tally up your scores. If the NEGATIVE column
outweighs the POSITIVE, it should strongly indicate
to you that this person has toxic tendencies, and is
therefore a negative influence on you.

This very simple technique won't work in all
circumstances. If you're dealing with a manipulator,
for example, they might say one thing to your face
and say or do something completely different behind
your back.

I appreciate this isn't a fool-proof method, so I've
listed some other things to consider. If it helps, you
can mark these questions 'yes' or 'no'. The more time
you answer 'yes', the more likely it is that you're
dealing with a toxic person.

**Do you feel drained of energy after meeting this
person?**

**Do you feel angry, hopeless or resentful after
meeting them?**

Do you leave them in a bad mood?

Do you dread meeting them?

Do you get the sense that the person doesn't like you?

Is the person quick to insult you?

Do they make you feel inferior to them?

Do they put you down in front of others, but dismiss their comments as 'only joking'?

Do you cry after meeting them?

Do they make you feel stressed, nervous or tense?

Are you snappy around them, or easily agitated?

Do you feel that whatever you do or say, it will never be good enough?

Do you rack your brains about what to talk to this person about? Do you have regular awkward silences in your conversation?

Do you feel freer and happier when you don't see them?

Does the prospect of never seeing them again fill you with joy?

Are you cautious about what you tell this person?

Do you feel as though you can't be yourself around this person?

Do you find you strongly disagree with this person's views and opinions?

Do your meetings with this person usually result in you arguing?

Do you feel that it's pointless trying to communicate with this person?

These questions, along with the exercise above, are designed to help you realise how much of an effect the person's negativity has on you. They should show you how easily – and quickly – toxic behaviour can spread to you.

When you looked back at the conversations you had, did it make you think about your own behaviour? When the person was bad-mouthing your friend, did you join in and agree with her? Did you do or say anything that disagreed with her negative attitude, or did you go along with her?

It's very easy to blame others, but sometimes we need to take a hard look at ourselves – our actions, the decisions we make, and the people we choose to have in our lives. We'll do this in detail in Part 2.

For now, let's continue to hone your skill at identifying toxic people by looking at how they can affect us.

A turd in the punchbowl

Do I really need to tell you how bad for you it is to allow toxic people in your life? You should never underestimate the power and influence toxic people can have on you.

People are highly susceptible to toxicity. Although it's not always visible, toxicity can do us serious damage – both physically and mentally. It doesn't matter how physically or emotionally tough you believe you are – we're all capable of being caught out. If you allow any sort of toxic behaviour in your life, it can spread very quickly. From becoming seriously ill to losing your job, it is no exaggeration to suggest toxicity can completely destroy your life.

Toxic people will make a good time bad, and a bad time terrible. Arguing and bickering is the norm for them, and anybody in their vicinity will get a regular taste of it. You may overcompensate by staying silent, or becoming defensive and reacting with venom to everything they say. However you act, they'll bring out the worst in you, and you won't feel as though you can relax and be yourself.

Have you ever been in a good mood, and then met the wrong person? I bet they completely destroyed your good mood. Catching a bad mood is contagious – just like a common cold. Your mood drops, and your energy levels drop with it.

You've probably already met a toxic person, so you'll know how bad it can be. Maybe you're reading this because you want to do your best to avoid someone – clever you! Either way, I'm going to offer you a sharp reminder of how toxic people can affect you by highlighting their influence in all areas of our lives.

Toxic people in relationships
Sharing your bed with a toxic person is probably the most dangerous thing you can do – especially if you're female. Allowing a man access to your body makes you very vulnerable.

Allowing a toxic person access is basically telling them that they have rights over you and your body. This is why toxic people are often physically abusive. If one day you decide that you're not going to allow them access to you, a toxic person will find it difficult to accept. In his eyes, you are his property, and he can do what he likes with his property.

If a toxic person becomes attached to you (and they will if you make it easy for them by putting up with their behaviour), the harder you'll find it to distance yourself from him. In extreme circumstances, he might start to stalk you. Thanks to social media, stalking doesn't necessarily mean parking on your street and physically stalking you. Stalking can take place as easily as checking a mobile phone or checking your online behaviour. This is another fundamental reason why you need to be extra careful when it comes to who you decide to be intimate with. Nobody goes into a relationship thinking they will be stalked – and it is rare. You don't have to be paranoid and view everybody as a potential stalker. But you should become more aware and cautious, so you can limit your chance of being affected.

We react more strongly when something means a lot to us. In other words, the deeper the emotion, the stronger the reaction. Is there any deeper or stronger emotion than love? Love makes us do all sorts of stupid things, doesn't it? Most of these things are harmless. They might result in you looking like a fool in front of your crush, or saying something completely out of character. For toxic people, however, they might not be so harmless.

It's not always your choice (or fault) if somebody falls madly in love with you. Love at first sight really happens. But it is up to you to decide who you fall in love with. 'I didn't press charges because I love him' doesn't cut it. It may well be true – maybe you do love him – but what about yourself? How much do you love you? No relationship is worth abuse. A toxic partner knows that as much as you and I, but if you allow their toxic behaviour to continue, they won't stop.

You should love yourself more than you love anybody else. If you value yourself, and you're in a toxic relationship, you'll soon realise you deserve more.

We'll cover more about what to do if you're in a toxic relationship in Part 3, but you might find you get a lot more out of a relationship just by improving how often and how well you communicate. Many relationships break down because of poor communication alone.

If you're in a relationship, you probably want things to work out. Things begin to change for the better, including relationships, when we educate the other person by communicating clearly and openly with them about the things we're not happy with. Too many of us rely on telepathy, and believe the other person knows what's on our mind without us having to spell it out. The book *Men Are From Mars, Women Are From Venus* is popular for a reason. Getting to grips with the fundamental differences between the sexes is a never-ending, but fascinating, journey!

Nobody will know what you're thinking until you start communicating. Strong relationships, including intimate ones, last because of strong communication. Toxic behaviour may flourish in a relationship that is lacking in communication. Is there anything worse in a relationship than going to bed on an unresolved argument and waking up in the morning with the same feelings of anger and resentment? Sulking and ignoring (both types of passive-aggressive toxic behaviour) continue, until this becomes a regular occurrence – and ultimately a toxic relationship. With a bit more communication, most arguments can be resolved.

Toxic friends

Most people have experienced a friendship turning toxic. There are lots of reasons why this could happen, and we'll cover a few in a second.

Being hurt by a friend – somebody you love, trust and rely on – is painful. If you've got years of history with the person, it can feel as though all of it has been thrown down the drain in an instant. None of us like change: when we realise somebody close to us is no longer good for us, we know our relationship with them has to change – or end – and we are often resistant to this.

But here's the deal about friendship – *people change*. That means the person you knew five years ago is not the same person you know today. Your mate who used to love partying every Thursday, Friday and Saturday night might now prefer to stay in with a takeaway and a good film. If you're still a party animal, it could cause your friendship to turn toxic, because you have grown apart and may not have as much in common. If one of you isn't strong enough to admit you no longer have much in common, there is likely to be a lot of backstabbing and toxic behaviour going on.

And the same goes for you. You are not the same person you were five years ago. People need common ground for a friendship to last. Friendships fade and people grow apart, and it's not necessarily anybody's fault – these things happen.

Growing apart is natural, which is why it pays to keep meeting new people. The law of attraction says that however you're feeling when you meet someone, whether positive or negative, you'll attract that sort of person in your life. Whether you believe in the law of attraction or not, this is common sense. Negative and cynical (toxic, if you like) people tend to attract other negative and cynical people, and positive and optimistic people tend to attract other positive and optimistic people. This makes sense because, generally, one can't stand to be around the other.

If you fall out with a friend and you share the same circle of friends, your other friends might not know who to side with. You don't need to concern yourself with this because, as I just pointed out, the people who are meant to be in your life will be there. You may find out that more than one of your friends is toxic. If this is the case, they'll naturally stay together, because that is the type of behaviour they are happy with. You should take comfort from knowing that, when you move on, you'll find plenty of other like-minded people who are on your wavelength. There are plenty more fish in the sea, as they say.

We're all guilty of indulging in a bit of gossip and backstabbing every now and again – it's human nature. Just look out for friends who show signs of the toxic behaviour I listed in the chapter on Toxic Traits. You should be particularly wary of narcissistic behaviour, such as a friend wanting you all to herself. If they show signs of jealousy towards others, it means that your friend might believe they own you: you are her property, and nobody else is entitled to spend time with you. Becoming somebody's property rather than their friend brings all sorts of problems. You have to show your friend that you are nobody's property, and that it's up to you who you have in your life. If a toxic friend can't handle that, read Part 3 of this book to find out what you can do.

A friendship should be judged by asking yourself one simple decision: Does the friendship add value to your life, or does it suck the life out of you? Here are a few simple questions to ask yourself.

Can you trust the person?
Can you confide in them?
Would they defend you?
Would they help you through a crisis?
Do they make you happy?
Do they support you, or are they jealous of you?

It doesn't matter how long you've known a person. If you answer 'no' to the above questions, they are not a true friend.

Friendship is a two-way street. A good friend will share their thoughts and feelings with you, as much as you do with them. If you're getting nothing from the friendship, and they're getting everything from it, it might be time to analyse why you're friends.

'Better the devil you know' isn't always the best policy when it comes to friends. Don't be afraid to review your relationships regularly, including your friendships. By doing this, you constantly grow as a person because you'll make more space for the healthier relationships in your life – even if they are new ones.

Don't be afraid to make new friends. When you're able to grow with the friends you've known for years, cherish them, and treat them well.

Toxic family members
When it comes to toxicity within a family, the net usually spreads far and wide. This is because dysfunctional behaviour tends to run in families. If your grandma was toxic, it's likely your mum is, and it's likely she'll have toxic kids, too. The toxic behaviour spreads so quickly because when you grow up with it, it seems normal.

Most psychologists believe that about 85% of families are dysfunctional in some way. So if you think you're the only one fighting a battle with your family, you're most definitely not! It still astonishes me today how many people have toxic family members, particularly toxic parents. Several books have been written on the subject of toxic parents alone, which gives you a good idea of how common it is.

When you're a kid, your parents are your God. If they behave in a dysfunctional way, your God is showing you how to behave. The way they choose to live their lives is your bible. If you're seven, you don't have much choice about how to live your life. And when you're old enough to make decisions for yourself, you've already been influenced by the people around you. It's this influence that is shaping your decisions and, in effect, your life – until you decide to stop and re-educate yourself.

It is no coincidence that the therapy and counselling industry is booming. Waiting rooms are filled with people looking for answers to why they've been treated so badly – especially by their parents.

Being treated badly isn't always obvious. It doesn't always mean physical abuse by a parent. It could be a parent giving their child too much responsibility, taking away their chance to enjoy being a kid. It's a heavy burden to be responsible for holding your family together at any age, let alone as a twelve-year-old. In this scenario, it's common for a child to suppress their thoughts and feelings because they don't want to burden an adult with more potential hardship. The obvious problem with this is that the child will grow into an adult who doesn't feel comfortable expressing their feelings, and that is likely to lead to poor mental health, and issues such as anxiety and depression.

The thing that toxic parents seem to neglect the most is love. There are many reasons why this might be the case, but I hope, if you're reading this, you'll agree that there is no excuse not to love your own child. There is no good reason to treat a person you brought into the world with disdain. I understand that no child is perfect – and kids can be pretty annoying and relentless! However, children depend on their parents for love and protection. There is no excuse to treat an innocent child in a toxic way.

Sofia messaged me about her experiences as a child. When she was thirteen, she was spotted as a model and signed up by a top modelling agency in London. For the next few years, she juggled schoolwork and modelling. Modelling work kept coming in, but it meant lots of travelling. Sofia began to feel the pressure mount up, and fell behind at school. She confided in her mum, who just told her to get on with it. She reassured Sofia that schoolwork wasn't important, and advised her to concentrate on modelling.

Sofia's mother pushed Sofia hard. She decided to take charge of every aspect of Sofia's life, including everything she ate. It's healthy and normal for teens to want to eat ice cream and other treats, but if Sofia even suggested eating something 'unhealthy', her mother would be quick to remind her how 'fat and useless' that would make her.

Aged sixteen, after three years of trying to manage schoolwork, modelling and her mother, the pressure got too much for Sofia. She developed generalised anxiety disorder and anorexia. Some days she wouldn't eat anything at all. Within a few months, she had lost three stones.

Her modelling agent had spoken to Sofia's mum about her concerns, and suggested that Sofia find help straight away. Her mother reassured the agent that everything was fine. Because Sofia was naturally shy, she found it difficult to confide in anybody – especially her mother, who didn't listen to Sofia, instead dismissing her problems.

Things only changed when Sofia fainted at school. Her teachers insisted on a meeting with Sofia's mother, and persuaded her to allow Sofia to have counselling. Unfortunately, there was a long waiting list. Still adamant that counselling was unnecessary, Sofia's mum was reluctant to pay for private counselling – even though the school had advised it.

Sofia continued to lose weight, and got more ill. Her mother began to resent Sofia because she couldn't do any modelling. Her resentment was purely financially driven.

When Sofia turned eighteen, she was entitled to access the bank account that held all the money she had earned from modelling. Her mother demanded that she have full access to it, but this concerned Sofia because she knew her mother was heavily in debt due to her extravagant spending habits. She knew if her mother got access to the money, she would waste it all.

Sofia wasn't working and wasn't well. She needed the money until she could get back on her feet and start working again.

Sofia offered her mum a set amount of money for helping her previously, but when Sofia refused to give her mum full access to the account, she kicked Sofia out of the family home and ended contact with her.

Although it was painful at the time, this turned out to be one of the best things that had happened to Sofia. When she was forced to find her own place to live, without her mother's toxic influence, she began to look after herself better. She started eating more, and doing the things she had previously enjoyed – such as going to the gym – without her mum dictating all her actions. She ate ice cream with her friends, and socialised more often.

She is now in her second year at university. She has limited contact with her mum, which at first was hard. But she came to realise that limited contact worked best, even though she felt loyal to her mother, who would frequently remind her that 'blood is thicker than water'.

A toxic mother will often point out: 'I gave birth to you so you'd better show me some respect!' In her mind, the fact that she gave birth to you means that you are her property, and therefore she can do and say as she pleases. A toxic father might want you to run errands for him, like nipping to the bookies to place a bet for 'your old dad', or going to the shop for cigarettes. There's nothing wrong with that, I hear you say. But what if you're six years old, barely able to cycle across the road on your own?

Many toxic parents don't do much to help their children's development. They are too busy living their own dysfunctional lives to care or worry about their children's lives. Fridges and shelves go empty, with vices like alcohol and cigarettes taking priority. Other types of toxic behaviour are demonstrated (there are too many to list here), that ultimately result in the underdevelopment of the child. Because the child lacks attention at home, he might seek attention by becoming a bully himself. If toxic behaviour is all he's ever known, he'll see it as normal.

Toxic siblings come in all shapes and sizes. The most common are older siblings who enjoy tormenting and bullying their younger siblings. They may call their siblings by cruel nicknames – just the mention of the name might cause you a panic attack as an adult.

Jealousy is also a common toxic trait between siblings. A lot of resentment can be shown to a sibling who has achieved something, especially if the sibling has been viewed as having an advantage – like being Daddy's pet. If the toxic siblings are resentful and underachieving, they won't respect the fact that a lot of work and effort might have gone into the achievement. It's easier for them to treat their sibling as the 'one who got it all' and believe they got nothing, rather than be proud of their sibling's achievements. Unless, of course, they were getting something out of the relationship – like money.

But kids aren't always innocent when it comes to parents and toxic families. You can be the best parent in the world and have a toxic child.

As I mentioned, if a child is brought up by toxic parents, it shouldn't be any surprise that they are demonstrating toxic behaviour themselves. But it's not always that straightforward. Toxic children may be influenced by people outside the family home – the media, celebrities, reality TV, the internet, school and their peers. This makes it difficult to control.

Denise sent me a message to say she was at the end of her tether with her daughter, who was seventeen. Growing up, she had a stable environment, and didn't want for much. They lived in a quiet village, and her daughter went to a good school. Denise worked hard to make sure her daughter came first, and prioritised her needs over hers – making sure she attended all her weekly hobbies, including horse riding and stage school.

When she turned fourteen, Denise's daughter started to rebel. She met a girl a little older than her, who was clearly not a good influence on her. Denise's daughter started to bunk off school regularly, and started to smoke and have sex. (Denise found all this out by looking at her social media messages.) All these things aren't unusual behaviour for a teenager, but Denise's concern grew as her daughter's behaviour become more rebellious.

Based on her research and on her daughter's behaviour, Denise suspected that her daughter had started to take drugs. And that's when things started to get much worse.

When her daughter stayed out all night without telling Denise where she was, she was crippled by worry. She would stay up all night, pacing up and down, consumed with anxiety. When her daughter finally came home, she wouldn't tell Denise where she'd been. When Denise asked, she was lucky if she got two words out of her. Her daughter would storm past her, give her a look as if to say 'don't bother', and go straight to her bedroom. Short of Denise locking her daughter in the house, she didn't know what else to do. She felt as though she had lost all control.

Denise was a single parent, and her ex, her daughter's father, was in the army. He was stationed in Germany, and the best he could do was try to talk some reason into his daughter over Skype. His daughter would just placate him, and promise him her behaviour would change.

Denise had met a new partner, and the relationship had been going well for about six months. That was when her daughter tried to sabotage the relationship by making up stories about how he was having an affair with one of Denise's friends. The accusations were completely unfounded but, along with the pressures and strains that Denise's daughter put on the relationship, he decided that he couldn't make the relationship work, and ended it.

Is there an argument to suggest that Denise gave her daughter too much when she was younger, including too much love? Is that possible? Was it because her daughter didn't have her father in her life for long periods of time, and she resented that? Was she cross about her mum being in a new relationship? Did she not like sharing her mother's attention with somebody else? Did she meet the wrong people, and was she too easily influenced by them? I don't know the answer to any of these questions.

Sometimes, trying to work out why toxic people behave the way they do does more harm to us, which is why it's best not to dwell on it. All you can control is your behaviour and your reaction – and we'll cover that in Part 3.

Toxic carers

I've spoken about toxic parents and families, but we shouldn't forget about toxic people who are carers and guardians as well. Carers and guardians are people responsible for children outside their parents' supervision, and they include teachers, social workers and foster parents.

When I was seven, my mum had a breakdown, and I spent time in foster care. It was one of the worst experiences of my life.

My foster parents weren't nice people. They prioritised their two children over me and my little brother – we were made to feel like outcasts from the day we got there. We'd sit down to eat dinner, and the kids would sneer at us. If we came into the living room to watch television, they would slam the door shut and lean against it so we couldn't get in. For two vulnerable kids aged four and seven – who already felt uncomfortable at the prospect of living with unfamiliar people – it wasn't the best experience. For a child, feeling like an outcast is as bad as it gets.

There is no doubt that some parents shouldn't be parents. But accidents happen. Carers and guardians are the worst type of toxic person – because they actually sign up to look after kids.

The same goes for toxic teachers. I know teaching is a very stressful job, and I have a lot of sympathy for teachers, but there is no excuse for telling a kid that he'll never amount to anything, no matter how angry or stressed a teacher may be.

When my geography teacher held me back in detention to tell me I'd never amount to anything, it created a memory that still burns today. Maybe he was having a bad day. I know I wasn't the best-behaved kid in the class, so there is no self-pity going on here. I'm simply pointing out that it's worthwhile thinking twice about what we say to kids – particularly vulnerable ones. A bit of guidance, education and patience, and somebody taking the time to show that they believe in the child (such as a teacher), can transform a young life. Telling a kid they're going to do great things will affect them as much as telling them they won't amount to anything – and we all have the power to do this.

Toxic people in business

The title of this chapter – 'a turd in the punchbowl' – is a good example of how one toxic person alone can completely ruin a business.

That lovely-looking punchbowl with the colourful and vibrant fruit floating in the refreshing punch – the one you can't wait to drink – is absolutely ruined by the floating turd. The turd doesn't have to be big; it just has to be there. It's enough to put anybody off! (Unless you're filming an episode of *Jackass*.) If you haven't already guessed, here, your business is the punchbowl, your staff are the fruit, and the turd is the toxic person.

Tom contacted me to tell me about an experience he had with one of his staff. Tom runs a manufacturing company – a small business, employing about twenty-five people, of whom about twenty work on the factory floor. Tom was heavily involved in the business, and was responsible for its day-to-day operations. It meant that most weeks he worked twelve-hour days, six days a week.

Wanting to spend more time with his family (after worrying that he was running himself into the ground and needed more down-time), he decided to employ a right-hand man – a production manager who would oversee the factory workers and make sure things were run properly in Tom's absence.

After advertising and interviewing three people for the job, Tom employed a guy called Pete. (Meet exhibit A: the turd in the punchbowl!) Pete had a solid background in similar production roles, and had managed larger teams than the one Tom was asking him to manage. To Tom, it seemed like employing Pete was a bit of a no-brainer.

Pete had left his last role a few months earlier, so was available immediately. Acting on impulse (because of his desire to free up his time), Tom asked him to start the next day – without following up on his references. (Tom's first big mistake!)

Pete came on board, and initially made a good impression. Notably, he reduced a few costs and fired some employees who weren't performing well. Tom was so impressed that he didn't bother following up Pete's references at all. Pete had convinced Tom he'd made a good choice, so what was the point in checking references? He didn't need to check to make sure Pete was a good guy if he could see it for himself, right? (Imagine the sound on *Family Fortunes* when the survey says X!)

However, Pete soon began to turn up to work late – especially on the days Tom wasn't in to supervise. Tom only found this out when he got a call early one Saturday morning from one of the production staff to say the factory was locked and he couldn't get in. (You probably guessed that Pete was meant to open the factory that day.) It's not the crime of the century, though, right? Mistakes happen, and people accidentally sleep in, don't they?

Tom, being a forgiving soul, thought that was all that had happened, so he called Pete to find out where he was. He got no answer, so Tom had to get up (on his only day off) and get down to the factory to open it up himself.

On the way he tried calling Pete a few more times, but still got no answer. As he approached the factory, his Saturday staff were waiting to be let in. Tom got out his car, got the keys from his pocket and unlocked the factory door. He opened the door and his jaw dropped. The factory had been emptied. Everything had been taken: products, machinery, computers – everything.

At this point, Tom, for obvious reasons, grew suspicious about why he couldn't get hold of Pete. His suspicions were justified when he sat down with the police to look at CCTV footage. It was later proved that Pete, and a few of his merry men, had used a couple of company vans to rob the factory in the early hours of Friday night.

It also came about that Pete had lied about his previous employer, and hadn't actually worked for the previous eight months. Can you guess where he was instead? That's right, you got it – he was imprisoned for robbery.

The moral of the story: always do background checks, and don't take shortcuts.

This, of course, is an extreme example of how a toxic person can destroy your business. But there are plenty more examples, and an employee doesn't need to rob you blind to make sure your business will fall apart if toxic people work for you.

All it takes is one turd in a factory, office, call centre, shop, restaurant, or any other place of work, and that stink will spread like wildfire!

The odds are that, in your working career, you've dealt with at least one toxic colleague – and I'm sure you have many a fond memory of them (if you're not currently working with them). Gossiping, back-stabbing, lying, sabotage – just a few of their toxic traits. Maybe you've had a direct taste of it yourself? If you did, you know that it stings. It can be enough to want to make you quit your job and not turn up again – which is why, as a business owner or boss, it's something to be very aware of.

Talking about business owners and bosses, when it comes to the workplace, we cannot forget toxic bosses.

Toxic bosses

My first experience of a toxic boss was in one of my first sales jobs after I left school. At seventeen, I started working as a car salesman for a large car dealership. Right from the get-go, I could see that my boss didn't like me. The fact he had to be persuaded to employ me in the job interview by his colleague was a clue. And if that didn't give it away, he also told me, during the interview, that he didn't like me. I should have walked away then, but I was young and naïve – and wanted to earn some cash – so I took the first offer that came my way.

In the end, employing me was a good decision, because I ended up being the top sales person in the entire group. Even though my sales massively bumped up his sales figures, he still couldn't get over the fact he didn't like me. I think me being young and outselling all the other experienced sales people got his back up even more.

Looking back, his toxic behaviour is clear to me, and I can laugh about it now. But at the time, it wasn't nice. When I was negotiating with clients he would intentionally stand within earshot, ready to shoot me down at any opportunity. He would belittle me in front of other staff members, and make comments about my appearance, including my hair, which I used to spike with hair gel. As I parked the cars in the forecourt, he would stare at me with his beady eyes and tell me to do it again if a car was a millimetre out of place. Rather than praise me for my sales, he'd remind me I was only as good as my last sale, and if at any point my sales dropped, I should forget about coming back in.

The peak of his toxic behaviour came when I was in his office when he got a call from his boss. I couldn't hear his boss's part in the conversation, but it couldn't have been a nice one. He slammed down the phone and, with venom in his eyes, told me to 'Get the fuck out of my office, otherwise I won't be responsible for what I'll do to you. And don't let me see you for the rest of the day!' He was a lovely guy, really – I must remember to send him a thank-you card. It's people like him (and experiences like this) that have made me the person I am today.

If you've had more than three jobs, the chances are you've bumped into a toxic boss. Toxic bosses are common because when you give somebody who might be pissed off a bit of power, it goes to their heads, and that tends to manifest as toxic behaviour. And the person who bears the brunt of it is the staff directly 'underneath' them.

To a toxic boss, being 'underneath' doesn't just refer to pay scale or company structure. You are below them in every way possible. They think that gives them the authority to do what they please, and say what they please. If you don't like it, they will be quick to dangle the prospect of you becoming jobless in front of you. They think, 'Put up with I'm dishing out, or go and find yourself another job. But I know you probably won't do that because it's not easy, so it looks like you're stuck.'

Having said this, I'm going to start out by showing a little sympathy for toxic bosses. This is because I've been a boss and managed teams of people, and I know it's one of the hardest jobs in the world. It's very easy to get pissed off with people in a working environment, which means it's easy to become toxic towards staff.

When your company is screwing you (if you're having to work a lot more hours than contracted, or forced to do a job that you didn't sign up for), the easiest target is your staff. This is no excuse for toxic behaviour, however. And I'm sure you have no sympathy if you're currently a victim of a toxic boss.

I've heard many stories – about toxic bosses who have destroyed people's lives, about toxic bosses who have had people fired because they simply didn't like them. In every story, one thing is common: people with a toxic boss hate them. They take their hate home, and because you're not able to call your boss a complete 'c' word to his face (here's a clue: the word isn't clown), they take out their frustration on their partner or kids. And that's not fair on anyone.

I know a lot of readers will have picked up this book because of a toxic boss. Part 3 explores some options for how to deal with them, but here's the most effective strategy.

When it comes to toxic bosses, there really is only one way to deal with them, and that is the direct approach. You have to deal with them head-on. Toxic bosses are generally bullies, and you have to show a bully you mean business. The company you both work for should shelter and protect you. In everyday circumstances, this isn't the case. That means you stand a good chance of success if you tackle your bully head-on.

So what do I mean by 'head-on'? You have to be direct and confrontational. When he talks to you as if you're useless, and nothing more than a piece of dirt on your shoe, ask him: 'What makes you think you can talk to me like that?' Be calm – you don't need to be aggressive. You just have to show him you're prepared to stick up for yourself.

Like most bullies, if you show him you're not going to put up with his behaviour, he will stop. When he appreciates he can no longer bully you, you might see him show you a new respect. He'll likely vent his frustration on another victim – somebody he knows he can bully and who won't confront him.

If his behaviour continues, you could also inform him that you're tracking and recording everything he says and does to you that you find inappropriate, and you will be going to his boss and HR (if the company has a human resources department) with it. If this doesn't scare him and show him that you mean business, he has deeper-rooted issues. See Part 3 for more options.

Toxic neighbours

I've added a section here on toxic neighbours for two reasons: (1) I have had toxic neighbours (as you'll soon find out), and (2) they're common, and can be the cause of a lot of stress and suffering. It's not an exaggeration to say that a toxic neighbour can destroy your life. Not being able to live peacefully in your own home is as bad as it gets.

I'll let you decide whether it's unlucky or me attracting negative energy into my life, but I had toxic neighbours three times in a row. On each occasion, I decided moving away was the best action. It sounds extreme but, once you hear my story, I'm hoping you'll have sympathy!

The first neighbours turned out to be swingers. They regularly had other couples over who 'shared their company', in the house and in the garden. Oh, and the husband also beat his wife up on a regular basis. We used to hear the abuse through the wall. It was particularly sad when the police showed up and were sent packing because 'There's nothing going on here, officer'.

My second neighbour enjoyed having sex with teenage girls (he was in his fifties) loudly enough to wake up the rest of the street. I hear you men saying 'Good for him' and 'You're only jealous'. But if you're being kept awake every night by the howls of a teen (and not teen) wolf, including slapping sounds and chain rattles (I'm not exaggerating), you'd get annoyed too. Plus, he liked to work on his car late into the night. It was a nightmare. It was clear his toxic behaviour wasn't going to end any time soon.

My third neighbours were just as lovely as the first and second. When I moved into the house in the winter, all was well and peaceful. That was, until the sun came out and, just like animals waking up from hibernation, they started throwing all-night parties. They would invite all their friends to join them in heavy drinking and drug-taking sessions. (The smell of weed from the garden was strong enough to knock out a large mammal.) When the police went around to ask them to turn down their music, they would happily comply, until five minutes after the police had left, and they'd just turn the music back up again.

Eventually, after two years of tormenting the entire neighbourhood, they were evicted. Although eviction was good for us, it just moved the problem family to another area!

I haven't experienced much worse than a toxic neighbour. There is something about their selfish attitude towards others that drives me insane. I just can't get my head around how anybody could be so selfish and thoughtless.

Anyway, rant over! My point here is some people will always be toxic – no matter what you do – including toxic neighbours. We'll explore all the options to resolve issues with toxic neighbours in Part 3.

Bullies

Whether you're being bullied or abused in a relationship, by a friend or family member, in business, at school or college, by a neighbour, or by a boss or colleague at work, the same toxic behaviour and traits apply. Toxic people behave in pretty much the same way, and this happens for the same two reasons:

1. You allow the behaviour to continue.
2. They need to feed.

We'll discover how to deal with bullies in Part 3 but, for now, think of a toxic person as a leech needing to suck blood. Just like a leech, a toxic person needs to feed off somebody's hardship and suffering. They grab on and don't let go until they're so full they drop off, or you burn them off.

That need can happen anywhere. If you allow it in any area of your life, it will continue to permeate into other areas. Before you know it, you'll have a ton of leeches on you, all having a good suck. The obvious problem is, you only have a limited supply of blood to give.

If you want to survive, you have to discover your true self. In Part 2, you'll discover why.

PART 2: DISCOVERING YOUR TRUE SELF

Serve notice

Now you recognise the traits and behaviours of toxic people, including how they can affect your life (if you needed reminding), now what? Are you going to allow their behaviour to continue, or are you going to do something about it?

My aim is that you no longer put up with toxicity. Before we move on, I'd like you to serve notice. Just like you decide to quit a job that is no longer good for you, I want you to quit toxicity.

You can serve notice however you like. You can say it in your head. You can read it out loud on a daily basis, to reinforce your decision. You can even print it out and put it in a place you often look at, such as your fridge or car dashboard. It's your choice. And here's how the notice goes.

To Whom It May Concern

I hereby give notice to anybody who wishes to continue treating me in a disrespectful, violent or abusive manner.

I will no longer tolerate any kind of mental or physical abuse, whether that is bullying, harassment, intimidation, controlling or manipulation.

Any such behaviour will result in me detaching myself from the person and situation, unless they make an effort to rectify and improve the circumstances. If the behaviour persists, I will inform the relevant authorities and do what is necessary to protect my welfare.

I have come to this decision because I know I deserve more. This behaviour makes me deeply unhappy and has a serious effect on my mental health and well-being.

I am no longer willing to live a sub-standard life dictated by others.

Yours sincerely

The new badass me

Eagles don't soar with pigeons

I called Part 2 'Discovering your true self' because I know everybody has strength in them – strength that they often don't know they have.

In the *Independent*, I recently read a story about how an eight-year-old boy helped his father when a jack fell from the car his father was working under. The car crushed his dad, preventing him from breathing. The boy, who weighed about three and a half stone, managed to jack the car off his father – lifting the same weight his father and older brother, aged seventeen, had struggled to lift together. The boy said that 'angels' had helped him do it. You don't have to look far to see many other stories of people who have managed to defy the laws of physics – and the odds.

Strength doesn't just mean physical strength. When I talk about discovering your true self, I'm mainly talking about mental strength: the capacity to make important decisions and stick to them, and the strength to know that you can handle anything that comes your way. This is your true self – the power within you that might be covered up by feelings of weakness (caused by toxic behaviour). When these feelings are lifted, your true self can shine through.

Whether or not you know it, or appreciate it, you possess great mental strength. I know that because you're reading this book right now. You've been through shit, but you're still here. That means you have already demonstrated the type of mental strength I'm talking about. You have handled what has come your way – and not only handled it, but you know you want something better.

You have great power within you – or, as I call it, 'an eagle'. Allowing your eagle to fly free and discovering your true self requires a few things, and one of them is understanding that you are your environment.

You are your environment

I don't need to meet you to know who you are. I just need to meet the five people you spend the most time with, because you're the average of these people. If I met these people, I'd have a good idea of who you are.

How do you feel about that? If you're reading this, it means you have at least one toxic person in your life, and that means you're being influenced by at least some level of toxicity (depending on how toxic that person is). Add another toxic person into the mix, and the toxicity level just rose significantly. Add a third or fourth, and you're reaching boiling point.

I'm not going to go into what you need to do here yet – I'm saving that for Part 3. The intention here is to get you thinking. I want to start preparing you for the changes you might have to make, because these changes are big ones – including changing the people you have in your life.

Do you think it is any coincidence that successful people have successful friends? Do you think it is luck that toxic people attract other toxic people? It is neither luck nor coincidence. It is common sense, and best summed up by the saying, birds of a feather flock together.

Birds of a feather

Why don't eagles soar with pigeons? It's because pigeons can't soar as high as an eagle, right? You can look at a pigeon and say that they don't have the physiology of an eagle, so it's not possible for them to soar. You could say that the eagle would be more likely to eat the pigeon than soar with it.

I'm using this example for a few reasons, because I want you to imagine yourself as the eagle, and anybody who is choosing to treat you in a toxic way as a pigeon. It's highly likely a toxic person will consider themselves a powerful eagle rather than a weak pigeon, but the fact that they are toxic means they are a pigeon.

People all have different advantages and disadvantages, such as social status and environmental influences (the environment we were born into). But there is one thing that we are all capable of, no matter our advantages and disadvantages – and that is *self-improvement*. We can all wake up and decide that we want to be a better person. We can educate ourselves quickly by opening a book and reading it. NO excuses! The library is full of free books, and we always make time for things we *want* to make time for. That means, unlike a pigeon, we can go from flying low (living a sub-standard life) to soaring above the clouds (living the type of lifestyle we know we are capable of achieving), whenever we choose to.

This is why you shouldn't feel guilty about leaving toxic people behind. If they decide to stay as pigeons and you want to soar as an eagle, that is their choice, not yours. What is *your* choice is whether or not you decide, as an eagle, to continue flying with pigeons. If you do, you have to be aware it might mean that you are, in fact, a pigeon yourself.

You might have known people for years, or even decades, and through education and self-improvement you've discovered that they are toxic and no good for you. There is no doubt that these type of long-term relationships will be the hardest to break, but it is a necessity. There is no other option. Eagles don't soar with pigeons. Successful people don't live with unsuccessful people. Happy and positive people don't allow cynical and negative people to influence them.

If you're not comfortable with leaving the pigeons behind, my advice is not to try. Don't punish yourself by believing that you can be an eagle and comfortably stay within a group of pigeons. The pigeons will gang up on you, and you'll soon be an outsider, and made to feel like a leper. Protect yourself against that by getting into the mindset that change is inevitable – or stop trying to change.

Are you suggesting I should only be around positive people, and I should ditch all the negative ones?

I want to go back to some earlier points here. Nobody is perfect, and we all have bad days. Everybody is capable of demonstrating toxic behaviour. It's people who demonstrate toxic behaviour _on a regular basis_ that you need to remove from your life – the ones who look to deliberately hurt you or destroy you.

Negative people are not always toxic. There are some highly successful and influential people out there, who could do you and your life a whole lot of good, who don't have a permanent smile on their face. They might naturally have a miserable and direct personality. That does not necessarily make them toxic. If they consistently demonstrated toxic behaviour (as listed in 'Toxic traits'), and used them with the intent to destroy, that would mean they are toxic.

You'll find that many successful businesspeople have a ruthless element to their personalities. If they didn't, they probably wouldn't be as successful as they are. This might make them smart and give them an edge; it doesn't necessarily make them toxic. If you want to be a successful businessperson yourself, it would be naïve to think that you have to be nice all the time.

Defining toxic people requires common sense. If you need a reminder, go back to 'Toxic traits' and do the exercise (The Negative Effect). Ask yourself the questions I listed – that will give you a clear idea of whether or not you're dealing with a toxic person.

Most of the time, identifying a toxic person will be easy. It might have taken a bit of education or a kick up the backside to realise it but, however you come about it, taking action is key. Being aware of a toxic person is one thing – it's taking action and dealing with it that will change your life. That's why it's essential you read Part 3 of this book!

Playing the victim

If you class yourself as a victim, stop. As long as you continue to class yourself as a victim, you'll always be one. Toxic people feed off victims, so from this moment, *you are no longer a victim*. You're a person who has gained experience and, based on that experience, you have learned valuable lessons. That is not a victim. That is somebody who has decided that they will no longer allow the past to define who they are – somebody who has decided to change the future.

Listen – we all make mistakes. Sometimes, before we know it, we've allowed the wrong person into our lives. Sometimes we have to learn the hard way before it really starts to sink in. But now it's time to stop playing the victim. We can't afford to keep making mistakes. We have to take action and change – and stop playing the victim.

It sounds a little harsh, but I need to give you a wake-up call here. The only reason you're playing the victim is because it's easier – it's easier to get bullied than it is to face up to the bully. (At least, that's what we think at the time.) But the situation you're in right now is only going to get worse if you're not dealing with it (by playing the victim). In the short term, it might seem easier to be a victim and put up with the behaviour, but over the long term it will do considerable damage to your mental state and well-being.

Playing the victim is no good for anybody. It's *not* easier, so stop pretending it is. It's time to start facing up to your demons. The alternative is misery, and a sub-standard life in which you allow things and people to continually dominate you and get on top of you. You know there is more to life than that.

Every time you believe you are not in control, you are handing your power to somebody else. So when you say things like, 'I can't cope with this person' or 'She drives me crazy', you are being a victim. You've handed over all your power to that person, because you're allowing them to dictate how you feel. Being a victim means you allow others to destroy your inner peace. You should be the only person who defines how peaceful you are – nobody else. Don't let somebody else change how you feel.

If you insist on being a victim, nothing will change. You're better off putting this book down and going about your business as you always have. However, if you hate the fact that you're a victim and want to do something about it, then we're in business.

As we move forward, I'd like you to continually reaffirm that you are no longer a victim – because you're not. Not in my world. You're only a victim if *you* choose to be a victim. You have a choice, and I'd like you to make the right one.

Setting your standards high

I know it's not easy to face up to this, but the fact remains: you're allowing toxic behaviour to be present in your life. No matter your circumstances, I know this is true for two reasons: (1) everybody has a choice, and (2) there will be somebody in the same or very similar position to you who is dealing with the situation differently. In other words, they're not putting up with it. You can look at physical, financial, social or any other advantage they might have, but I'll guarantee there is an example of somebody dealing with toxicity who isn't as advantaged as you. So what makes them different? Quite simply: *standards*.

We all live by a set of standards. These standards dictate who we have in our lives, and how we allow them to treat us. If your standards are low, you'll accept that being abused is just part of life. If your standards are high, simply a hint of abuse from somebody would be enough for you to call it a day with them.

When I say standards, what I'm really talking about here is self-respect. How much do you value yourself?

Compromise can sometimes be very dangerous. As soon as we let our standards slip, we go backwards. We let people into our lives we shouldn't and, before we know it, we've got a whole bunch of people in our lives taking advantage of us.

Don't get me wrong. Standards are incredibly difficult to maintain. When faced with a tricky situation, it can be easy to drop our standards and settle for second best. That's why people with high standards have something in common. They are willing to make sacrifices for them, and do whatever it takes to uphold them.

Low-level consciousness

What separates humans from animals is consciousness – our ability to be aware, and conscious, of the decisions and actions we make. Toxic people operate from a low level of consciousness. In other words, they put very little feeling or thought into their actions (they are thoughtless). That's why, when dealing with toxic people, we need to take a lesson from the wild.

In the wild, if you're weak, or perceived to be weak, you get eaten. If you don't get eaten, you become the pack leader's lackey. He'll loaf around all day while you go out hunting for his dinner.

Seeing as we're no longer playing the victim, or accepting ourselves as weak, you have a few options. You can continue to be a lackey – and accept the fact you'll always be one. You can challenge to be the pack leader, which will end up in a fight you might lose. Or you can operate at a new level of higher consciousness, get out of the wild, and join a new pack. You can decide that being a lackey or fighting are beneath you and, with your new level of higher consciousness, choose the option that best suits you.

In this instance, doesn't joining a whole new pack – a pack that won't treat you as a lackey or as food – sound like the best option? That's definitely the option an eagle would choose.

It's not personal

In a lot of circumstances, when a toxic person is treating you badly, it's nothing to do with you personally. It's everything to do with them, not you. You can't control others. You can only control yourself.

If somebody is making you feel like shit, it's because they feel shitty themselves. Toxic people have a great way of transferring their feelings to others. Seeing you in distress makes them feel less shitty about themselves. It's a power trip.

Why beat yourself up wondering why they do what they do? You'll probably never know why they choose to behave the way they do. You wouldn't want to understand what goes in their head – that might make you just as bad as them. Just remember that happy and secure people don't bully others.

If you have to understand why a toxic person does what they do, it comes down to *significance*. The reason social media is so popular is because of our need to be seen as significant. The need to be wanted and noticed is wired into humans, and if we feel as if we're being neglected (or have been neglected in the past), we'll look for significance in any way we can get it.

This can lead to toxic behaviour. For example, how significant do you become to somebody if you point a gun at his head? You suddenly go from being insignificant to the most significant person in the world. Not all toxic people point guns at people's heads, of course, but the way they seek significance will come out in many other different methods. The more you put up with and accept these methods, the worse they'll get.

If you're being affected by a toxic person, stop beating yourself up, thinking 'Why me?' or 'Maybe I deserve it'. It might simply be a case of being in the wrong place at the wrong time. Remember: there is no situation that can't be changed or resolved.

Nobody is perfect, including you or me, but nobody deserves to be bullied or abused in any way – no matter how somebody might have made you feel, or how much you've been convinced otherwise.

When you detach the 'why me?' mentality from the situation, it makes it less personal. Of course, it doesn't make it acceptable, but if you accept that it's not personal – it's not your fault – you'll be able to handle it better.

Sometimes you have to look at handling a situation as making a business transaction. If you get wrapped up in emotion, you tend to feel guilty when you shouldn't, and a toxic person will make the most of that. They will use your guilt against you, so you give them another chance (probably the fifth chance you've given them). They will pull out every trick in the book and use every heart-rending statement they know will affect you.

'Don't leave me. I'll be lonely.'

'Who will go to the shop when I've got no food in the house?'

'If ten years of friendship means nothing to you...'

'Will you come to my funeral?'

'If you leave, I'll kill myself.'

When you make change your priority, by deciding you deserve more, you will be manipulated. You have to toughen up, stop being a victim, and stick to your guns. Remember, you're doing what you're doing for the sake of *your* welfare and well-being. And if you want things to work out between you and the other person, somebody has to be strong enough to break the pattern.

You can only control your actions, not the actions of others. Remember that you can handle any situations that arise from your decision. You were tough enough to make it, and now you have to be tough enough to see it through. The alternative? You continue to play the victim, and nothing changes.

Forgive – but don't forget
When I talk about dealing with toxicity being your choice, I'm referring to you being a responsible adult, capable of making decisions and taking action.

When you were a child, you were innocent. You didn't have the ability to be responsible and make decisions. As a five-year-old, you couldn't pack your stuff up and leave. You were completely dependent on your parents or guardian to look after you, love you, and protect you. If you were treated badly as a child, it was not your fault.

If you've been affected by toxicity from a young age, you might grow up believing you don't deserve anything more. You might hate other people, and have a desire to hurt them – like you've been hurt. You might blame yourself for what has happened to you, and this will create a victim mentality.

As you know, a victim mentality won't get you anywhere. It's time to be an eagle and let go. Let go by forgiving yourself, and others.

Forgive yourself for anything you believe was your fault.

Forgive yourself for the times you thought you could do more.

Forgive yourself for the years of hurt.

Forgive others for the hurt they caused you.

Forgive others for the times they called you names, and told you 'You're not good enough' and 'You will never amount to anything.'

Forgive others for the times they got joy from your misfortunes.

How does it make you feel when you harbour hate? It's not a good feeling, is it? There is no power or joy in harbouring hate, holding a grudge or seeking revenge. Toxic people do it because they're toxic. They are pigeons for the same reason, and not eagles.

There is a big difference between forgiving and forgetting, and forgiving – but not forgetting. If you forgive somebody and let go of the hate, you don't have to suddenly pretend that everything is OK. You don't have to forget all the times they treated you badly. You're forgiving them for your *own* well-being, not for theirs.

Letting go of the hatred releases *you*, not them.

Carrying toxicity around with you makes you no different to them. It will keep you caged up like an animal. Set yourself free and forgive – just don't forget. Learn from the past, and never suffer fools lightly again. Set yourself free and forgive, but don't make the same mistakes again with the same people.

Learn from the past

Albert Einstein's definition of insanity is doing the same thing over and over again and expecting different results. How many times are you willing to give a toxic person a chance? How many chances should you give? It's a good question, with no definitive answer. The answer depends on the person and the situation. More importantly, the answer should be based on how you feel.

Katrina sent me a message telling me that, a few days previously, she had walked in on her husband in bed with another woman. What makes this scenario worse is that Katrina was days away from giving birth to their second child. And it wasn't the first time her husband had had an affair – he'd had at least two other affairs before (that she knew about).

What sort of person has sex with another woman, in their family bed, when his partner is days away from giving birth to their child? A toxic person, of course! I was sickened to find out that, after this, Katrina had given him yet another chance, and they were trying to fix the situation.

I completely get the fact that things aren't always black and white. In this instance, Katrina had a baby on the way. The thought of being a single parent with a new baby and a toddler probably scared her more than the prospect of living with a cheat. But allowing fear to drive her decision will put her into the mindset of a victim.

How soon will it be before Katrina's husband is unfaithful again? If his behaviour is consistently forgiven, what else do you think he might do in the future that he would expect to be forgiven for? Do you think it would bother him if he passed a sexually transmitted disease on to Katrina? I doubt it.

You can, of course, argue that Katrina shouldn't have had another baby with him, given his history, but she did. There is nothing she can do about what has been done. She can only change what happens in the future. In this instance, she would be insane to assume that her husband will ever change. Therefore, she should get some self-respect and tell him to do one! Allowing fear to dictate her decisions, by being scared about the prospect of being a single parent, will only keep her trapped as a victim. The future may well be scary for her, but it's no scarier than what her toxic partner could do to her in the future.

It angers and astonishes me how many chances toxic people are given. Like a misbehaving kid, if a toxic person isn't told to stop their behaviour in a firm and direct manner, they won't stop. They'll continue to behave in exactly the same way they always have, and the person on the receiving end of their behaviour will continue to be a victim.

What you choose to do from this moment forward will shape your future. If you continue to give toxic people more chances and play the victim, you will always be a victim. Instead, stop! Reclaim your self-respect and make a different decision. Think like an eagle, and either eat those pigeons, or leave them behind.

You've changed

As you progress on your journey of detoxification, you'll naturally leave toxic people behind. You'll attract more positivity in your life, and things will look brighter, cleaner and fresher.

Because the past has a habit of haunting you, you might be tempted to go back to your old ways, including seeing the people who were no good for you. These people will say things like 'You've changed'. You'll be thinking *I didn't work this hard to stay the same*, but your frustration will keep you silent.

You might smile and, out of politeness, ask, 'What do you mean?', but you won't want to know the answer, for two reasons. (1) You already know you've changed – you've worked to achieve everything you've done, and (2) you don't care for the opinions of somebody who has never made any effort to improve themselves, and resents the fact that you have.

Not allowing yourself to be dragged back by the past means understanding why it might happen, and that's what I want to educate you about here – to make sure all your hard work isn't undone.

Breaking the system
Whichever part of the class system you were born into, it was cleverly designed to keep you there. For me, coming from an underprivileged working-class background, the system was designed to keep me underprivileged and working-class. A lot of the behaviour that was around me was toxic. My neighbours regularly fought, burned-out abandoned cars were plentiful, and us kids were out getting up to no good.

Breaking out of this system was no easy feat. I'd say I only managed to do it about ten years ago. That was when I started to educate myself properly on the importance of wealth, health and well-being. These things were never taught or considered a priority, at home or at school.

This isn't a book about success or failures in the UK education system. This is a book about toxic people, so what does all of this have to do with it? I'm simply making the point that it doesn't matter what situation, class, or environment you were born into; you can still become an eagle if you wish.

The more you make excuses about your past, including how underprivileged or unlucky you are, the more you're fuelling the fact that things will never change for you. There isn't a situation or circumstance that can't be changed!

The best example of somebody overcoming adversity is a guy called Nick Vujicic. Nick is an Australian motivational speaker and best-selling author, and one of the most inspirational people I have ever seen.

Nick was born without limbs, but he has lived a more fulfilling and active life than most people. He surfs, he drives, and he has a wife and children. Nick's experiences, including being bullied at school to the point of wanting to commit suicide, led to him dedicating his life to helping others. He visits schools and talks to groups of people about the importance of loving yourself, no matter what anybody says. Nick is a perfect example of somebody who had an ideal excuse to grow up hating the world and everyone in it. Instead, he chose a different path, and now his love and compassion have reached millions of people across the globe.

Nick defied the odds. He tells everybody who might look different or act different to the norm that it's OK to be different. He gives people the strength to know that if they're being bullied, they can do something about it. He reinforces the fact that there is only one opinion that counts – yours.

You too can break the system, and defy the odds. Whenever you might be feeling ungrateful or stuck, I want you to remember Nick. If he can do it, so can you. If I can do it, so can you. If all the other people in a worse situation than you can do it, so can you.

The past does not dictate the future

If you come from a toxic family, dysfunctional behaviour would have been the norm for generations. No social status or class is immune to dysfunctional behaviour; it's just that they demonstrate the behaviour in different ways. Not even the Royal Family can get away from scandals, including affairs, bribery, rehab and Nazi costumes (to name a few).

If you're sitting right in the middle of a toxic family tree, one of the hardest jobs you're going to face is getting out of it. Roots go deep, and the past will always be there to haunt you. At every turn, people from the past will try to draw you back in. They will do their best to suck the life out of you, and disrupt your progress.

Toxic people will not want you to succeed. As pigeons, they will look up at the sky and watch you soar. They won't watch in admiration – they will resent the fact that you have moved forward. They won't want to join you. Instead, they will want to clip your wings to bring you back down to their level. They'll do it using all sorts of tactics, including saying and doing nasty things that are intended to get a reaction from you. As soon as you give them a reaction, they know they've caught you. And once they have you snared in their net, you'll find it harder to escape.

You have to deal with the past just like you deal with anything else that poses a challenge to you and your welfare. It's inevitable. There is no point trying to run from it, hide from it, or pretend the past doesn't exist. Like all problems, you have to face it head-on. Otherwise, it will continue to haunt you.

If the past comes knocking, it's up to you to choose which methods from Part 3 will suit the situation best. The most important thing is to remind people from your past that you are no longer the person they knew. You are no longer a pigeon. You are an eagle.

Where possible, leave the past where it is – in the past. The past is the cause of most of our stress and anxiety, so it's best left behind. The same goes for worrying about the future. Nobody can predict the future, so there is no point worrying about what might happen. The only thing that is real is this moment, right now. We all have more power and control over our lives when we live in the now.

When you find yourself worrying about the past or future, draw yourself back to the present by allowing yourself to sit down, close your eyes, and take five. Even eagles have to take a break.

Speak out

A significant part of your change may be you talking about how you feel on a more regular basis. It's common for people who have been subjected to toxic behaviour to internalise their emotions, which means suppressing how they feel. This leads to them not talking or sharing their thoughts with anybody.

Toxic people depend on this suppression – especially in cases of abuse, where they don't want other people to know what's going on.

Speaking out is essential for many different reasons, but the most important is your health. When you internalise how you feel, it produces stress hormones that can be detrimental to your health. This can cause a number of health issues, including heart disease, heart attacks, strokes and cancer. It's no coincidence that people in highly stressful jobs get these types of illnesses regularly. Dealing with toxic behaviour could cause the same level of stress as being in a full-time job, which should indicate to you the effect it may have on your health.

I used to internalise everything. I remember suppressing my feelings ever since I was a small kid. It was my coping mechanism for dealing with stress. I didn't want to add hardship to the people around me by expressing how I felt, so I kept it to myself. The trouble was, I got very good at it, and continued it until I was an adult. The result was being regularly ill and living with crippling anxiety for over fifteen years.

Don't allow the same thing to happen to you. Talk regularly about how you feel, and don't internalise your feelings. If you struggle to talk in depth to the people closest to you, find somebody impartial, such as an experienced counsellor. Keep sharing and talking, and don't be afraid to say what's on your mind.

The worst in you

Toxic behaviour has a habit of bringing out the worst in you. You'll find yourself acting in a way that doesn't represent you at all – you might even feel ashamed of how you're acting. Some of the behaviours you might demonstrate include:

- going silent
- reacting angrily to everything that's said
- taking offence easily
- being difficult
- sneering
- making backhanded comments
- being miserable.

If you find yourself acting like this, it's likely that you're around somebody who is demonstrating toxic behaviour towards you. These behaviours are because of the feeling of insecurity you get around toxicity. Because you feel so uncomfortable, they act as a coping mechanism, protecting you from the fact you don't want to be there. They are also a reaction to the fact that you expect change – that you are no longer willing to be a victim and, deep down, you know you deserve much better.

As your strength grows, you might find the best solution is not to be in their presence. You'll start to appreciate that it's up to you who you talk to, and when you talk to them. In the meantime, it's worthwhile having a think about who you feel uncomfortable around, and why that might be the case.

Making a fair judgement
Is there a valid reason for you not liking somebody, such as the person obviously being toxic towards you? Is it instinctive – you just don't have a good feeling about them? Is it reactive – you just don't like the look of somebody?

It's important not to overanalyse, or judge a book by its cover. Not liking somebody without a valid reason for your feelings makes you no better than a toxic person. If you have this type of mentality, you'll find it difficult to form relationships with most people. Give people a chance, and then form an opinion of them based on their actions.

If you're meeting somebody for the first time in, say, a business environment, you won't have long to form an opinion of them. If it's unlikely you'll meet this person again, your opinion won't matter as much. If they're demonstrating lots of toxic behaviour in the short time you meet them, they'll be out of your life after your meeting, so you don't need to worry about them. Be patient, and remember that you won't have to suffer them for long. If you stand to get something out of the meeting, putting up with a bit of toxic behaviour for a short period of time might be worth the investment.

The people closer to you deserve more of your patience, including your fair judgement. Friends, family and work colleagues are the people you spend most time with, so they therefore have a greater influence on you and your mood. Everybody has off-days, and all of us are capable of acting toxic, including you. Putting somebody in the 'toxic' category because of an off-day is an unfair judgement. It's important not to forget the two key signs to look out for: *consistency* and *intention*. Are they consistently demonstrating toxic behaviour, and is their intention to destroy?

Have you ever met somebody and instantly formed a negative opinion about them, only to be proved wrong once you got to know them? People deserve a fair judgement: otherwise, the person quick to judge is likely to be doing it unfairly, and is therefore, themselves, demonstrating toxic behaviour.

A lose–lose situation

You simply can't win with toxic behaviour. If you keep trying, you're only going to become more frustrated and disillusioned. No matter how much common sense should be involved, you'll keep hitting a brick wall – and you'll feel like banging your head against it.

If you are smart, funny, witty, charming and/or attractive, a toxic person will hate you for it. Their jealousy will eat them up inside. They simply won't accept the fact that somebody else might be more intelligent, likeable or attractive than them. They will also hate you if you're a failure, and will slate you for being useless. So, like I say, it's a lose–lose situation.

There is little point trying to please a toxic person. The truth is, they may never like you. They may never accept the fact that you have changed. That is their choice. You should focus on pleasing yourself. You can do that by accepting and loving the person that looks back at you in the mirror. You'll not only have fewer disappointments, but you will be much happier.

You'll stop being run by false beliefs – things that might have been drilled into you for years – like how useless you are, or unattractive you are, or how thick you are, or how you should live your life, including what clothes you should wear, what you should eat, what job you should do, and how you should spend your time and money. When we're told things like this for years, we end up believing them. And toxic behaviour, in the form of manipulation and bullying, is usually the cause.

There is a sense of great freedom to be had from detaching yourself from the need to please others –

including not accepting their negative views towards you. When you learn to appreciate that only your opinion counts, you go through life with an extra layer of armour. Although it's invisible to the naked eye, it will make all the difference to you.

PART 3: DEALING WITH TOXIC BEHAVIOUR

Detoxifying methods

We all deal with different types and levels of toxicity. I don't have a magic answer for you all, but I can offer tried and tested techniques for how to deal with toxic behaviour.

Sometimes one method will work. Sometimes you have to try more than one, more than once, to make sure a successful detoxification has taken place. It all depends on the results. (By 'results', I mean how much your happiness and well-being increase.)

Going back to the chocolate factory example I used earlier in the book, if the company is to be sure that its products are free of toxins, it needs to test and test them again to make sure. The company will get rid of the old contaminated stock and start again. It won't put products in the shops and see if they make customers ill. It will make sure the problem is resolved before allowing the products to be sold.

Toxicity isn't always easy or straightforward to deal with. Sometimes it permeates into areas you didn't expect it to. The detoxification might require an extra strong dose or a lengthier treatment. Whatever it needs, just be reassured that, with the right treatment, any situation can be changed – and improved.

My advice is to try all the methods I list, and stick to what works and feels comfortable for you. Cutting people out of your life might be a step too far. Having a reasonable conversation with them might be unrealistic. The trick to your success lies in testing and testing again.

Communicate

We communicate with other people every day, so you'd assume we should all be pretty good at it. This is not the case. Most of us stink at it! Most of the time we don't say what's really on our mind, so we internalise our problems, making them seem a lot bigger than they are. When we do communicate, we lie – a lot – because we want to fit in and impress others. We might also lie because we're struggling to communicate exactly how we feel, because of nerves or a lack of self-confidence. What a complicated bunch us humans are!

So many relationships fail because of a lack of communication. If only we appreciated that telepathy isn't any good in a relationship, we might be able to save a few more of them! If there is something on your mind, you have to communicate it. Don't expect everybody else to know what's going on between your ears.

I used to be terrible at this. From a very young age I'd internalise everything and wouldn't say what was on my mind. I think it's because my mum had enough going on in her life that I didn't want to burden her with any more, so I kept quiet. Unfortunately for me, the result was crippling anxiety and depression that lasted through my teens and into early adulthood.

Sometimes I wonder how different my life would have been if only I had spoken what was on my mind. It's not something I suffer with any more – as you can probably tell. The difference between how I feel now, and how I felt then, is immense.

If you have a problem, communicate it. If there is something on your mind, communicate it. If somebody is making you feel like crap, communicate it. You don't have to be rude or obnoxious, as a toxic person might be. You don't even have to communicate it there and then – you might want to save it up to tell a trained professional, such as a counsellor. But don't leave it too long, and be confident enough to get it off your chest – however you do it.

Abraham Lincoln was an excellent communicator and leader of people because he never criticised anybody. He famously said 'Judge not, that ye be not judged'. In other words, treat people as you would like to be treated yourself. If you don't want to be judged, don't judge others. If you don't want to have toxicity in your life, don't act toxic yourself.

Have a reasonable conversation

It's not always possible to have a reasonable conversation with a toxic person – for the obvious reason that most toxic people aren't reasonable. Trying to have a reasonable conversation with a toxic person is like trying to have a conversation with a tiger in his cage. You go in with an agenda, including what you want to say, and all he's thinking about is how good you would taste. However, as I mentioned before, most problems, whether in relationships, with a boss, or with your kids, come about because of a lack of reasonable communication.

If you want to develop the ability to deal with toxic behaviour, then as well as communicating, you need to be reasonable. Fire does not put out fire. Forget about how a toxic person might act – you have no control over that. You only have control over you and your actions. Because you're the bigger person (the eagle), you can act in a calm and sensible manner, no matter how enraged and angry a toxic person might be towards you. If you act in the same manner as they do, what makes you any different?

If you find that having a reasonable conversation doesn't work, no matter how many times you try, don't torture yourself any longer. All it will do is bring out the worst in you. In this instance, no communication is the best solution.

No matter how much you want to get through to the person, if they are not open to communication, it's pointless. They aren't open to the very thing that is essential in any healthy relationship, and a relationship can't work unless you are able to have a reasonable conversation and see each other's point of view.

Analysing why a toxic person might not be able to communicate won't do you any good. Just accept that there is always a reason. Be the bigger person by being the one able to move on and get past the behaviour that isn't good for either of you. If a toxic person chooses to weigh themselves down with pettiness, spitefulness and revenge, you can't control that. You only have control over yourself.

Confront the toxicity head-on
How brave are you? How brave have you been in the past? If the answer is 'not very', it's likely that you haven't tried this option. It takes guts to confront toxicity head-on.

Humans are more likely to do something to avoid pain rather than to gain pleasure. That's why, if we're being bullied, for example, we will try to avoid the bully rather than confront him. The problem with this method is that the bully doesn't always go away. If you work with the bully, live with him, or go to school with him, avoidance isn't easy. A bully feeds off attention, and if you don't confront the problem your pain and suffering will continue, which is exactly what the bully wants.

The reason that dealing with toxicity head-on can be effective is because most bullies aren't used to being confronted. They're cowards at heart, and depend on intimidation and fear to keep you in your place. Sometimes the only way to overcome this is to face it, head-on.

What do you mean by 'confront'?

I'm not suggesting that you go and punch a bully in the face – now that would be naughty of you, wouldn't it? By confronting, I mean you should communicate how you feel. Like I mentioned above, I suggest that you verbally communicate, in a sensible and reasonable manner, how his behaviour is making you feel.

You might be surprised by how effective this is. It's common for long-term relationships to break down simply because of a lack of communication. We stop saying what's on our mind and expect our partners to be psychic and to know what we're thinking without us saying anything. Unfortunately, people are not telepathic, so this method tends to be unproductive. Communicating what's on your mind, and how you feel, can solve a whole range of problems – including those that you thought were unsolvable.

You need to use common sense when confronting toxicity head-on. In some circumstances, such as if you're being physically abused, it could lead to more physical abuse. If you feel you need support, you don't have to confront a bully alone. If you can, ask for help from a friend or family member. Counselling is also an option. A counsellor can act as a mediator, which (in some circumstances) can be very effective.

The other person has to be open to the idea of counselling too, of course. You could communicate the idea (or sell the idea) to them as follows:

'I love you and I think we have a future together. But we've got things we need to work out to make our relationship stronger, and we need help to do it. How do you feel about us going to speak to somebody to help us overcome the things getting in our way?'

This example is based on a relationship, but it can be tweaked to work with a friend or a boss. It is also very much dependent on an individual's circumstances. For example, in cases of abuse, joint counselling isn't recommended. If you have any doubts, you are always best to speak to a professional before deciding to take this approach.

If you do take it, you're instantly reassuring the other person that you love them and want to be with them. You're helping them recognise that there are problems that need to be sorted out, rather than being swept under the carpet and ignored. You're telling them it's not all one-sided, and that the problems are as much yours as theirs. When you ask 'how can we solve this?' you're asking an open question that requires a response. You don't mention the term 'counsellor'. This could scare people or put their back up. That's only going to result in them becoming defensive. You want them open to the idea, not closed off to it.

If you take this approach, be open-minded to all outcomes. If the person seems receptive to the idea, you're on to a winner. They might not want to hear what you have to say, to the point of being stubborn. They may dismiss it as a stupid idea. If their response is negative, don't allow them to convince you that counselling is a bad idea. A pigeon might view it as a weakness, but an eagle knows that looking and asking for help is never a bad idea.

Nobody said that facing a bully and confronting toxicity head-on would be easy, but is it any more difficult than having to deal with the toxicity for the rest of your life? I doubt it.

Make them aware of their behaviour
If confronting the behaviour head-on or trying to have a reasonable conversation does not work, you can make a toxic person aware of how they're behaving using subtler techniques.

One of these techniques is to mirror their behaviour. For example, if somebody is being intentionally bitchy, be bitchy back to her. Give her a taste of what she's dishing out. If she doesn't like it, she might begin to appreciate how her behaviour and words might be affecting others.

You can try the mirroring technique for most behaviour. For example, if somebody (such as a toxic boss) is intentionally overreacting to a situation to try to embarrass you, overreact in the same way. It can sometimes be the quickest way to get them to own and appreciate their irrational behaviour.

The mirroring technique is very much dependent on the type of person you're dealing with. It's optimistic to think that a toxic person will change their behaviour if they're confronted by it. Instead of make them appreciate how horrible they're being, it could just as easily wind them up more.

At this stage, it's highly likely that the toxic person is in a stronger place than you are, emotionally and mentally. If that weren't the case, you wouldn't be tolerating their behaviour. That gives them an advantage over you. It means that they might be quick to bat back anything you throw at them, including a mirroring technique. As a master manipulator, they will have you believing you're in the wrong, and that their behaviour and actions are reasonable. Plus, toxic people are generally stubborn, so you should expect a fight.

Acting in a way that is out of character may not suit you, and your tactics will become obvious to a toxic person if you suddenly begin to do this. Strength develops over time, so you might want to consider other methods first, then build up to mirroring. Try more subtle approaches, such as communicating how you feel – either directly to the person or by talking to somebody else (which we will cover next).

I'm not a fan of tit for tat, and I don't think lowering your standards to placate somebody else is the best course of action – especially for an eagle like yourself. This part of the book gives you lots of options to try and see what works for you.

Talk to somebody

A problem shared is a problem halved. When it comes to dealing with toxicity, this well-known saying is true. Dealing with a toxic person is incredibly difficult, but you don't have to handle it alone. There are people out there who can help.

Your first point of call should be your friends and family. Do you have somebody close to you that you can confide in and trust to share your thoughts and experience? Not everybody does, and this might be because the people closest to them *are* the problem. If you don't feel comfortable sharing your emotions with the people closest to you, you can speak to somebody impartial, such as a counsellor. You can start by speaking to your doctor, who will be able to recommend counselling services and organisations that can help. If you can afford private sessions, search for local counsellors online.

Whoever you speak to, somebody ideal is somebody who understands what it's like to deal with a toxic person. They might have been through it themselves, and can offer you some supportive encouragement and practical advice. We all need support at times; there is no shame in it. Don't suffer in silence.

If you need immediate help, there are phone lines you can call, including the Samaritans. If you go online, you can search for organisations that support people going through abuse, including domestic violence. Phone lines are usually open 24 hours a day. If at any time you don't feel safe, you should always contact the police.

Write a letter
My 'serving notice' letter is intentional. There is something powerful about writing your thoughts down on paper that can make you feel a whole lot better.

Grab a pen and paper, or your laptop, and start writing down how you feel. You can write it and address it to the toxic person, if you'd like. You don't have to give it to them. This can just be an exercise for you.

Writing a letter can be particularly effective if you're struggling to communicate with the toxic person verbally. If they choose to read your letter, it might hit home to them how much they are hurting you, and you might find they change. This will depend entirely on the toxic person, of course. Whether it works or not is no reflection on you. You are again demonstrating that you are the eagle – the bigger person who is willing to do what it takes to improve your life.

Toxic people can be intimidating, and will quickly shout people down. They can't do that with a letter. If you struggle to say what's on your mind, writing a letter gives you the time and space you need to say exactly how you feel. Again, whether or not the toxic person decides to read it is insignificant. If they don't, it shows you that you are wasting your time with them, and any more effort you take to resolve the situation will be pointless.

Whatever you decide to do with your letter, make sure you write down exactly how you feel. Get every thought and emotion down. When you're writing, think of it as your final opportunity to say how you feel. Write down each example and episode that has hurt you. Remember: this exercise is for you, nobody else.

Because this exercise is for your benefit, it doesn't have to be a letter if you have no intention of handing it over. You could simply write a list: bullet-point all the things that have been said and done that have hurt you and, underneath, write how they made you feel. This list might also come in handy at a later date when a toxic person has convinced you it was all your fault. The list will help jog your memory and reassure you that you were right.

The list isn't designed to make you stay angry and bitter. Don't read it every day and spit venom at it.

That's not how an eagle acts! It is there to help you get your thoughts and feelings down on paper, so you can reconnect with yourself and your feelings. It's a permanent record of how you felt on this date – and why. Look back at it at times of weakness, when a toxic person might make you question yourself and your sanity. Use it as a reminder of past events, because a toxic person will be good at convincing you that everything is your fault. The list will prove to you otherwise.

Think like a business

The best businesses make quick and decisive decisions. Sometimes these decisions are ruthless, made without thinking emotionally. Profit drives these decisions: without profit, a business wouldn't exist. That's why businesses deal quickly and decisively with anything that could jeopardise company profits.

Not all business decisions are fair. A company may have to make redundancies, and tell hard-working, loyal individuals that they no longer have jobs, for example. But if the business is at stake, staff will see redundancies as a necessary sacrifice for the future of the business.

I'm mentioning all this because sometimes, when dealing with toxic people, you need to think and act like a business. You need to take emotion out of the equation, and make a decision based on your own wants and needs.

You might be seen as too soft. This could be why you're being treated the way you are. If you weren't soft, you wouldn't allow anybody to treat you badly. Being too soft means you're putting lots of emotion into your decisions (unlike a business). These emotions are typically guilt and fear. If you allow them to, these emotions will govern everything you do. They'll keep you trapped and scared. Toxic people depend on this.

When you think like a business, you take away your emotion. You don't allow emotions such as guilt and fear to control you, because you know the decisions you're making aren't about emotion – they're about keeping your well-being intact.

If a business was driven by emotional decisions, it wouldn't be in business very long. If every decision was based on whether or not it might hurt somebody's feelings, the company would simply go out of business, because business sometimes means hurting people.

This may come across as heartless and ruthless. That's intentional. It's probably the complete opposite to how you think and feel. But that's what I'm trying to make you appreciate. Don't allow your well-being to go out of business.

Cut it out
One of the most effective ways to deal with toxicity is to cut it out completely.

Of all the methods in Part 3, this is the most challenging. Cutting out somebody who might be close to you, like a family member or friend, is not easy. If that person is dependent on you and vulnerable, it makes it twice as hard. It's likely the toxic person has come to depend on you. You are one of the very few people who puts up with their behaviour. If you decide (good for you) that you're not going to put up with this behaviour any longer, and you manage that by cutting them out of your life, you've just changed their world.

You might have been her meal ticket. Maybe you were his punch bag. You could have been the person he took out all his insecurities and frustration on – like when he'd had a bad day at work and you got the brunt of it at home. You were most certainly his lackey. That's a big hole to fill, and most sensible people won't be willing to step in to replace you.

Cutting out the toxicity is the most effective way of dealing with it. Out of sight and – eventually – out of mind is what you're after.

As I mentioned, there is no easy way of doing this. All you can do is be open and honest, and communicate to them why you've come to this decision. It is then up to you to make sure you enforce your decision by cutting off all communication, both on- and offline. As time progresses, the lack of communication and interaction will become a reality, and it will get easier for all of you.

You have to be strong. And you shouldn't feel bad. Did he feel bad when he was treating you the way he did? I very much doubt it. Eventually, he will always find others to spread his toxicity to.

Move
In most circumstances, moving away from toxicity should be a last resort. You probably have friends, family and a job where you live. Moving away to start over again isn't easy. Plus, it's not fair. Why should you have to move because of the behaviour of others?

Keeping your distance from someone is different to moving. It's similar to cutting the toxicity out. The more distance you can put between you and the toxicity, the better. If I decided to have a quiet drink in a bar, and all of a sudden a big brawl kicked off, I'd leave. I would rather leave than face the prospect of a chair landing on my head. By leaving, I'm putting distance between the brawl and me. Remember: proximity is power.

If somebody is violating your standards and values, how much more of an influence would they have on you if you saw them regularly, compared to never seeing them?

For example, if you have a toxic relationship with somebody, the more time you spend with that person, the more likely it is the relationship will get worse. If you have a toxic boss, they are more likely to continue to make you miserable if you have to report to them every day. That's why it's best that you either cut them out of your life completely, or limit the time you spend with them. This will very much depend on what the relationship is, who it's with, and how close they are to you (both in terms of distance and relationship).

Keeping your distance is about using common sense. If you have a toxic neighbour, for example, and they've been a problem for a while, maybe you should consider a move. If your experience is similar to mine with toxic neighbours, and you've tried to resolve the problem using lots of different methods but the problem is still there, moving might be the only option you have left.

Some of the first options you could try include speaking to your neighbour to voice your concerns (if you feel safe doing this). You could talk to your local council and make a complaint about anti-social behaviour. You could speak to other neighbours who might be affected and come up with a joint plan (there's strength in numbers). If at any time you don't feel safe, you feel threatened, or their behaviour is really anti-social (such as a party keeping you awake all night), call the police.

If you do move, don't jump from the frying pan to the fire. Do some research. You can never guarantee anything but if you do your research, you will at least limit your chance of making a mistake. Knock on the door of your potential new neighbours, and ask them what the area is like. Not only will you learn more about the area, but you'll also be able to suss them out. Park for a while in the street, at different times of the day and evening, and listen out for any noises or activity that might cause you concern. Do online research on crime rates. If you experience problems once you've moved in, revert to the above solutions.

If you decide to move house, it should always be with the understanding that you can't – and shouldn't – run away from your problems. Let me explain, because you might think moving is running away. Moving only counts as running away if you haven't explored all your other options first. If nothing works, then moving is a sensible option. Some people will always be toxic, and it's up to you to choose whether or not you want to be around that type of behaviour.

If you're moving away from toxic neighbours, you can simply move on. You have no commitment or emotional ties to them. But if you're in a relationship with a toxic person, for example, moving away without saying why is a form of running away. The situation will need closure; otherwise, your ex might be confused and may harass you.

Although your reasoning might be perfectly clear to you, it might not be so obvious to them. That means they will look for answers until they get them. That can lead to unhealthy behaviour or stalking. We will look at how to gain closure in the chapter 'Moving on'.

Take a break

Sometimes taking a break to put distance between yourself and a toxic person/situation can be a good solution. Coming away from the situation gives you time to think and reflect. Having the toxicity right in your face won't give you that opportunity.

This is not easy if you've got kids, a job and other commitments, I appreciate that, but if it is a viable option, it's one you should consider. If you do it, make sure you switch off your phone and don't check your emails. You'll get the clarity you need when you have no direct contact. If you are not available, after a period of time the toxic person might appreciate what they are losing. (You don't know what you've lost until it's gone.)

Some people will always be toxic, no matter what you do. Baseball bats, police, the council, and other methods sometimes just don't work. Sometimes distance is the only real solution. It is far from being fair, and quite frankly it pisses me right off to think that anybody is forced to move because of somebody else's toxic behaviour. But it is a solution, and one that you could try if you have exhausted all others.

Instant relief

Dealing with toxic people is one of the quickest and most effective ways to reduce stress and anxiety in your life. If you equip yourself with the tools you need to instantly deal with toxic behaviour, there is no way for it to penetrate your armour. Here are some of the most effective ways to get instant relief.

You can only control yourself; you can't control anyone else

A great source of frustration is the belief that you can somehow control or have influence over the toxic people in your life. If you haven't discovered by now, this isn't how it works with a toxic person. The more you try to influence them using reason, the more disillusioned and disheartened you'll become. Reduce your stress and anxiety by remembering you can only control you and your actions; you can't control anyone else.

Toxic people will do their best to control you and dictate how you do things, where you go, who you see and what you do. It's up to you to put them straight.

The more you do it, the more they'll get the picture, until they realise that trying to control you is futile.

If he's telling you he doesn't want you to go out with your friends, and there is no valid reason for this (apart from the fact he doesn't want you to do it), this is the type of controlling behaviour we're talking about. Some of your options are:

Agree with him and stay in: But expect nothing to change – or for things to get worse.

Go out earlier, for a shorter time: A gentler approach that is a compromise, and still conforms to his controlling behaviour.

Keep in touch when you're out: To show him that your relationship is still important, even though you have a life outside it.

Leave him: Because you refuse to be controlled.

You are in absolute control. If you don't want to do something, don't do it. If the terms aren't right for you, don't abide by them. If you don't like the options on the table, create your own option, or walk away.

If you're worried about the consequences of your disobedience, get more control by planning your moves and stay one step ahead. There is more of a consequence if you put up with whatever it is you don't want to do. The more you do that, the more your independence will slip away, until it's completely gone.

Not taking control – allowing things to go on as they are – will mean either nothing will change, or they will continue to change for the worse. You have to be willing to take charge of your life, your well-being and your mental health. Nobody else is responsible for these things. It's up to you to grab the baton and start running in a new direction.

Set boundaries

If you've been dealing with toxic behaviour for a while, it's likely that you haven't established boundaries. If you had, the problem might have already been solved. Not having boundaries gives toxic people a licence to treat you in any way they see fit.

Setting boundaries helps to define you as a person, and tells everybody else exactly what you're willing to put up with.

For people you know you can trust, your boundaries can be relaxed. We all need to let our hair down every now and again, and being around the people you trust will help you do that (another reason why surrounding yourself with like-minded people is healthy for you). For anybody you deem toxic in any way, put your boundaries back up. You may have to deal with toxic people regularly, and practising putting up your boundaries will help you.

Typical examples of putting your boundaries up include saying no to a toxic boss who regularly asks you to work late; cutting a conversation short when a toxic friend might be gossiping; telling a toxic parent to back off when they're still trying to tell you how to live your life (and you're 46).

To help set boundaries, imagine a fort that runs all the way around you. Maybe this fort has a moat. This is your boundary, and if anybody crosses it, either physically or emotionally, you will act to defend it. I'm not talking about violence here. (You'll discover why toxic behaviour doesn't solve toxic behaviour in the next chapter.) By setting your boundary (your fort and your moat), you're making it clear to anybody who wishes to treat you negatively that it won't be tolerated. Similar to setting your standards, you have a clear boundary that shouldn't be stepped over.

Unlike a real moat, toxic people won't fall into your moat, but you can guarantee they will try to breach it. It's up to you to decide what detoxifying methods will work best for that. It's also up to you to stay strong and not allow your fort to be taken over. If you decide that your boundary has been breached enough, and you decide to cut the behaviour out of your life, remember it's the toxic person's choice to be toxic. It's natural for you to feel guilty, almost as though you are abandoning them. You're not. You're becoming the best person you can be, and if that means cutting the toxicity out of your life, so be it. You've outgrown their behaviour, and it's time to move on with your life. You'll quickly get over this feeling because (1) you have nothing to feel guilty about, and (2) you'll feel much better afterwards.

Don't get sucked into drama, gossip and negative energy

Toxic people will always have some drama up their sleeve. The only way to avoid the drama is to not get involved in it. Distance yourself from it. Remember: proximity is power. You'll never be able to stop the drama so don't try. Just keep out of the way.

Gossiping about others is a usual pastime for toxic people, and that's a little harder to avoid because everybody likes a good gossip, making it easy to get caught up in it. Maybe you've been sucked in yourself? I know I have. It's incredibly difficult to break through the negativity of drama and gossip when it surrounds you. It can very quickly become your life and, before you know it, you're in the middle of something that doesn't involve you.

This is the law of attraction at play. The negative energy that surrounds toxic people draws in other toxic people, so it's common to find them in groups, and it's also common to find yourself being sucked in. Being sucked into the negative energy tends to bring out the worst in you so, where possible, steer clear of drama and gossip.

If you know you're dealing with a gossip, apart from avoiding them completely, you should make them aware that you're not interested in getting involved. If you have to, be direct with them. You don't need to be aggressive, just assertive: 'I don't think it's fair to talk about somebody when they're not here. Let's talk about something else.'

They'll get the message, and they'll either stop gossiping to you, or find somebody else who is interested in gossip.

Don't get into an argument
Talk is cheap, and words get bandied around when we argue. Arguments can quickly turn into a petty of war of 'he said this' and 'she said that'. It happens in all types of relationships every day, and I have no doubt you've got into such squabbles with your friends and family (toxic or otherwise).

Usually, you can get past these petty arguments, but there are times when you can't: when you're dealing with toxic people. If you're arguing with a toxic person, it's likely they'll do something that will push your buttons, such as use privately shared information against you as leverage. That's going to annoy and hurt even the most patient person.

It's hard to have a genuine, heartfelt conversation with a toxic person because they show little interest in how you're feeling. It's their way or the highway. When you're dealing with such an attitude there is little point in trying to reason. Getting stuck into a heated debate serves little purpose. All it does is fuel the anger further. You have to remember: in their eyes they are never wrong.

You simply can't win when it comes to arguing with a toxic person, so it's best not to try.

Kill them with kindness
Faced with toxic behaviour, it's not always easy being polite. But if you're in an unavoidable situation, like having a toxic boss, being confident and staying polite is your best course of action – certainly temporarily – until you can change the situation in the way you want to change it, not in a way that is forced on you.

Another circumstance might be you being in love with a toxic person, or loving a toxic family member. This will lead to a false sense of loyalty, and rather than you wanting to distance yourself, you might feel compelled to try to help them instead. In this instance, I commend your loyalty, but you need to be aware that a leopard rarely changes its spots. In other words, you're going to find it incredibly difficult to change a toxic person because ultimately, they are who they are, whoever they are and however close you are to them.

As I mentioned previously, the only way they will change is through education and awareness. If they're not willing to get educated or become aware of their behaviour, there is little you can do.

Whatever the scenario, be sure you are confident and polite with a toxic person. They will sense any form of weakness, and they will take advantage of it. Give them an inch and they'll take a mile!

By being confident and polite, you're not giving them any reason to take advantage of you and your good nature. They also have no good reason to try to negatively affect you with their behaviour. Like a bully, they will get bored and move on. Before that happens, they will dig their heels in and fight. If you are confident, you will have the ability to fight back. This means not lying down every time a toxic person decides to treat you negatively. You are more powerful than you'll ever know. You are an eagle. Confidence means taking this knowledge and using it.

Be aware of your emotions
A toxic person might not be able to control their emotions, but that doesn't mean that *you* can't. Be aware of your emotions, and when you feel your blood boiling, rather than have a shouting match that will get nowhere and resolve nothing, step away. Be the bigger person – be the eagle.

It's also important to recognise how a toxic person might be intentionally pushing your buttons. They probably know exactly what they need to say and do to get a reaction from you. Stay one step ahead. When you recognise why, when and how they are pushing your buttons, they will no longer hold any power over you.

They want you to become irrational, like they are. And making you angry by pushing your buttons is the quickest way to get you there. Irrational thinking and behaviour makes you no better than them. Stay aware of your emotions, and stay rational. That is what makes you an eagle and not a pigeon.

Externalise your emotions
Don't bottle things inside, including how you feel. Not only will things seem much bigger than they are, but you'll also become a ticking time bomb of anger, until one day you explode!

Let it all out by talking to somebody – a friend, a family member, a colleague, anybody you can have a chat with. Just getting it off your chest can make you feel a million times better. If talking doesn't work, go for a run or pummel a punch bag. Harness your excess energy and put it to good use.

Go for a walk. Leave the environment that is making you feel trapped. Take in some deep breaths, and get some fresh air. Leaving the scene, even if it's just for a few minutes, can give you the time and space you need to make rational decisions.

Don't forget your sense of humour
At times, it's incredibly difficult to keep your chin up and laugh, I appreciate that. But humour is such a powerful thing that it shouldn't be forgotten, even at our most challenging times.

Toxic people might not have a sense of humour, but that isn't stopping *you* from seeing the lighter side of life. And having a good laugh will let you do exactly that. Whatever is going on around you, put your favourite comedy show or comedian on, and have a good laugh!

Remember, don't take life too seriously. As soon as you do that, the weight of the world feels as though it's on your shoulders.

Humour can also be effective for breaking a toxic person's pattern. In the middle of a heated argument, the last thing they will expect is for you to use humour to lighten the mood.

If a toxic person is about to land a punch on you, cracking a joke probably isn't the best idea. Like a stand-up comedian, you have to get your timing right – to make sure you don't get heckled or get a bottle thrown at you. Getting the right level of humour with the right timing can soften even the steeliest heart.

Listen to music and watch videos

At the start of this book I mentioned that I watched motivational videos on YouTube and listened to music to help me through my dark days. What I didn't mention was how effective I found both of these things: sometimes, they gave me instant relief.

If you're going through a difficult patch, be sure to listen to music and watch videos. There is a reason why most people use music to change their mood. There is something about listening to your favourite tunes that can get you through the toughest times.

Whenever you need to, blast that Iron Maiden. (Or Enya, if you prefer.) However, be mindful of your neighbours – you don't want to be a toxic neighbour!

You could also listen to a podcast. Podcasts are great if you're busy and on the go. You can listen to a podcast in the car, at the gym, going for a walk – anywhere you can put your radio on or headphones on. There are some great podcasts to help you with motivation and improving your well-being. I've heard the Carl Vernon podcast is pretty good! You can find that and subscribe to it on iTunes.

Watch people who inspire you on YouTube – people who have been through what you have, or people who have experienced their own adversity, can inspire you to take action. My go-to people are Nick Vujicic, Tony Robbins and Les Brown. (You may also want to include me, of course!) I have all these guys accessible on my phone through YouTube, books, audio books and podcasts, making your phone the best and most accessible tool to carry with you.

Don't forget to take your headphones wherever you go, and you can get a daily dose of inspiration whenever you need it.

Keep a diary

For me, writing is one of the best ways to release tension and anger. There is something cathartic about getting your thoughts down on paper.

So grab a pen and paper (or your laptop), and get ranting! Scribble down all your thoughts and experiences, and get them out of your head.

Nobody has to see what you've written (unless you want them to), so you can say whatever you like. Write it down then rip it up, if you prefer.

I recommend keeping a private diary or journal of all your daily thoughts and experiences. At the end of each day, write down what has happened and how you felt about it. If you get used to doing this daily, you'll begin to reconnect with yourself and your feelings, and you might find it easier to say what's on your mind.

If nothing else, it will be something to look back on, and offer you a good read, further down the line!

Surround yourself with like-minded people

It's common sense, really – the law of attraction. If you surround yourself with negative, toxic people, it won't be long before the contamination takes effect and you become toxic yourself. It's very much the same if you surround yourself with positive people – you become more positive yourself.

If it weren't for some of the people closest to me helping me through some dark times, I'm not sure if I would be here today. You know the days I'm talking about – when you don't want to get out of bed, when you can't think rationally, and feel as though everything is on top of you. When you can't help but replay everything negative from the past like a broken record. These are the times you need like-minded people in your life – the type of people who can help you through the tough days and tell you that tomorrow is a new day.

It doesn't matter how tough you are, or believe you are, everybody needs good people in their life. If you haven't found that person yet, you don't have to go out looking for them. Instead, *be* that person for other people. In other words, if you want to attract other positive like-minded people, be a positive person. If you want more friends, *be* a friend. You'll probably meet new friends when you least expect to, but the timing will be just right.

Like-minded people tend to be on the same journey as you, and won't have the inclination to dictate to you how you should live your life. They won't act toxic towards you because, like you, they appreciate the negative effects this has – not only on others, but also on themselves. They won't be jealously looking at your yacht or criticising it – they'll be busy building their own yacht.

Sit on your luxury yacht and keep sailing on. Pass the sinking ships with a smile on your face, and only invite like-minded people aboard.

Focus on solutions, not problems

When something negative happens to us, we immediately think of the worst-case scenarios. When we keep following this pattern, it clouds our judgement and rationale, until we believe that nothing good will ever happen again.

We'll never meet the right person, so we might as well put up with the one we've got.

We'll never find a better job, so we might as well work for the same toxic boss.

We'll never amount to anything; the teacher was right.

People can be negative. Why is the news on every day at prime time? Because generally, news isn't news unless it's negative! Bad things happen in the world; there's no getting over that. But do you need to fill your head with constant negativity, including a daily reminder of how bad and negative the world is? (Try not watching the news for a week and see if you feel more positive.)

Or you could keep believing what toxic people are telling you. Keep believing that your life will never change. But remember: whatever you focus on, you're going to get more of. When you fixate on negativity, including all your problems, you create a negative response – usually in the form of stress and anxiety.

I know, deep down, you believe something else. (You wouldn't have got this far in the book if you didn't.) It's time to tell yourself a different story, one based on solutions and facts, not problems and the 'what ifs…' we fabricate.

There isn't a situation or problem that can't be changed.

When you focus on the fact that you can handle anything that comes your way, you'll focus on the solutions, rather than the problems. If you remember that you can change something by making a new decision, that will make you feel better instantly. The cloud will lift, and you'll take action, rather than being held back by negative and false beliefs. You'll feel positive, and your stress and anxiety will fade.

Quit thinking about how difficult your situation is to sort out. Instead, focus on what you *can* do. You'll have a new sense of control and a completely new demeanour. The next time you meet a toxic person, they will see in your eyes that you mean business and you won't put up with them.

Beware of trolls

Today, trolls don't live under bridges. They live in bedrooms with old pizza rotting in boxes, next to dirty socks lying on the floor and scattered empty cans of energy drink as they lean over their laptops with a pale complexion, bad posture and a fat gut. The Caps Lock button on their keyboard is heavily worn, and they often wear a wrist brace – thanks to too much typing, and other activities.

Unfortunately, as well as having many obvious good qualities, the internet has made it much easier for trolls to abuse people – and toxic people take full advantage of this. (Online, a toxic person is commonly referred to as a troll.) Rather than them having to get up and go out to abuse somebody, all they need to do is go to their bedroom, open up their laptop, and they're away. With a mobile phone, they don't even have to move. Using fake profiles and bogus email addresses, they can also troll people anonymously.

Online bullying, in the form of trolling, is so prevalent in our culture that I'm sure you've personally experienced some form of it, whether through social media or a bad online experience. We need to look at the ways toxic behaviour can affect us online – so we can be extra-vigilant in future.

The pitfalls of social media

The amount of toxic behaviour that goes on online is obscene. If you look at anti-bullying campaigns and websites, you'll see how prominent things like cyberbullying, cyber-stalking and trolling have become. A lot of it is to do with how easy it is. But many other reasons aren't so obvious, and social media has many pitfalls you should be aware of.

You might have heard the term 'FOMO', or fear of missing out. That's why so many of us can't stand to be away from our phones, even for five minutes. If we're not changing our status, checking our tweets, or watching funny cat clips, we're missing out. The invisible power social media has on us keeps drawing us back in – and this can be unhealthy.

This is one of the reasons I don't have a personal Facebook account. The temptation to watch videos of my neighbours' pets and my friends' perfect lives all day is just too much. I mention 'perfect lives' here, not to be callous (that would be toxic of me!), but for a reason. One of the most dangerous ways social media is used nowadays is to judge our own lives against others. This, along with FOMO, is why social media use can cause all sorts of problems, including anxiety and depression. A recent study conducted by

Anxiety UK showed that 51% of people polled said social media had a negative effect on them.

All of this comes down to the simple fact we never get the full picture. When you scroll through Facebook, you're only getting the highlights of other people's lives. You'll look at your own life and think, *why is everybody else's life perfect when mine isn't?*

I recently heard on my local BBC radio station that comparing our lives with others on social media is causing an epidemic of self-harm and anxiety. (If you've read *Anxiety Rebalance*, you'll know this is a subject I'm very familiar with.) Not only is the internet causing various psychological problems, but it's also behind a lot of toxic behaviour.

It's easy to become resentful towards others when we don't have the full facts. Don't be fooled! You might see pictures of your friends having a great night out, while you're stuck indoors watching the kids, but everybody else has problems too. Nobody's life is perfect. Someone posting lots of fabulous photos on Facebook may be dealing with problems far greater than yours. People just have different ways of masking their problems, and an easy way to do it is by posting online about how perfect their lives are: *At least others will think my life is great, even though I know it's not.*

Think of it like this. If somebody was truly blissfully happy, do you think they would need to plaster it all over social media to prove it to others? It's more likely they would be enjoying each moment in real life rather than needing to prove it to you, me or anybody else.

Of course, there is nothing wrong with wanting to share. But if you're more concerned about posting a perfect selfie on social media than you are about enjoying the moment, that needs to be addressed. If it isn't looked at, it could lead to toxic behaviour – both from you and your connections. You can end up developing narcissistic traits and forget about the things in life that are *really* important, such as living in the moment. That will have a knock-on effect on your health and your relationships with others.

The obvious solution to all of this is to limit your time on social media. I know that asking you to stop it all together would be like asking you to chop off your arm, so I'm not going there! All I'm suggesting is that you withdraw from it a little. Start appreciating that there is more to life than changing your status or tweeting. Enjoy meeting and having real-life friends, rather than posting and waiting for comments from hundreds of online 'friends' you may never have met. Live in the moment.

For your own sanity and well-being, be mindful about how social media might be influencing you and your mood. How do you feel after half an hour on Facebook or Instagram? If it's not making you happy, or it's creating toxic behaviour, either in you or others, wean yourself off it.

At lunchtime, when you get the urge to check your timeline, go and do something else, such as have a real-life conversation with somebody. You may find your life will improve, and you will start to build stronger relationships with people.

Online dating
Online dating (OLD) has become extremely popular in recent years for many reasons, convenience being a major one. It's so much easier to pick up your phone, flick through some pictures and swipe to show you like someone than it is to get to know somebody in the flesh by having a meaningful conversation with them.

Because I've only had two long-term relationships, both lasting over a decade, I've never had to use OLD. If I were single, I probably would consider using it. But I'd do it with one massive caveat: I would put my extra-thick toxic-people-seeking glasses on.

I've heard dozens of disaster stories from my friends about OLD. It appears to be much less reliable than finding your true love in real life. And I think I know why.

You don't know who you're meeting online. Anyone can post a photo taken from anywhere on the internet and say it's them. How do you know what's written in a potential date's OLD profile is true? Some OLD sites are used by married people looking for extra-marital 'fun'. I'm sure that some of you reading this will have an OLD success story. However, if you meet somebody online you know nothing about them. You don't know any of their friends or family; you don't know if they are who they say they are. This makes OLD more risky than dating somebody you know from work, through friends, or from a sports club you attend.

Would you employ somebody without checking his references first? No? So why would you date somebody based solely on a picture and information that they've provided – information that could easily be fake?

Do you think it's any coincidence that most decent, loyal and honest people are married and too busy working to be fishing around online for a bunk-up? And it's not just men. I know men get a bad rap when it comes to cheating and looking for a one-night stand (and rightly so), but it takes two to tango.

The online dating pool is swimming with toxic people, many of whom just want no-strings sex. If you meet somebody this way who turns out to be toxic, don't be surprised if things turn sour.

You may be lonely and want some company, but you already know how detrimental it is to get into a relationship with a toxic person. It might not have to get as far as a relationship. Sometimes all it takes is a date with the wrong person to know they're bad for you – another reason why vetting is so important.

If I had a pound for the number of times I've heard someone say, 'I just can't find the right person', but then realised that they kept looking for love in the same place, I'd be a rich man! It's like Albert Einstein says about the definition of insanity: doing the same thing over and over again and expecting different results. If you keep finding frogs online, your prince might be somewhere else. And that will require you to do something apart from focusing on OLD.

Think of new ways to meet people. Some of the best places to meet people are through your friends, at work, or by doing a sport, hobby or class. The latter means you're also meeting people who share your interests.

I don't mean to sound like a killjoy; I'm only concerned about your welfare.

Do you need a digital detox?
If you're online a lot, you might want to consider having a regular online detox. Your offline life, including taking care of your mental and physical health, will always be more important than your online presence. Here are some quick options for you.

Limit the time you spend online
As I said previously, limiting your time online is good for your mental health. Cyberbullying and harassment can only happen when you're online.

Shutting your laptop and turning off your phone are the most effective ways of dealing with it.

Block people

If someone is harassing you, you have the option of blocking them. You should never respond to their harassment. That's exactly what they want.

Remember: your attention is what they crave. Stop paying them attention, and they have no power. If you're worried about the consequences of blocking someone, remember that they decided to harass you, and they're not worried about how you feel. You can only control your actions, not theirs.

Watch what you share

It's important to be careful about what you share online, including on social media. Something as simple as a picture taken on a wild night out might persuade a prospective employer not to make you that job offer.

According to lifehack.org, in 2012 more than 12 million people became victims of identity fraud online. Fraudsters find out your name, date of birth, place of birth, job title, place of work, names of your pets, your interests and hobbies from your social media posts, and then use this information to access your bank accounts and hack into your online accounts. You should review your privacy settings on all your accounts.

It's important not to feel paranoid, but you also need to be safe. Before you post or share, be mindful of who might be looking.

If you're a parent, make sure your kids are safe by using parental filters wherever you can. You'll never completely know what your teenagers are up to, but ensure you talk to them regularly about what they're doing online and who they're chatting to. Make sure they feel they can speak to you if they encounter a problem online.

Speak to your ISP or phone provider
If you're receiving harassing emails, calls or text messages, you don't have to put up with it. Speak to your ISP (Internet Service Provider) or your mobile phone provider. They'll have procedures for this, and they will be able to advise you. Don't dismiss or ignore harassment.

If the emails, calls or texts are coming from an unknown source, your ISP can work with the police to track the culprits down. If the harassment is serious, you should always report it to the relevant authorities. Save all the emails and texts, take screenshots of messages, and record calls wherever possible. It will help the police investigate and find the perpetrators.

Change your phone number

'Hello, Mr X. Did you know you have an outstanding PPI claim and you're owed thousands?'

'Hello, Mr X. We understand you have been involved in a traffic accident and you're entitled to compensation.'

These are the types of cold call we all love, especially just as we're about to sit down for dinner. It's fun for toxic people (who haven't got anything better to do) to sign you up to all sorts of companies.

If you're being harassed in this way, and you're getting lots of calls, you should seriously consider changing your number. Nobody likes the inconvenience of changing their telephone number, but it's pretty simple to get a new one and tell people about it. The trick here is to be very selective about who you give your new number to.

As well as changing your number, you could choose to have more than one number. You could keep one number confidential, and only give it out to people you know you can trust.

Change your email address
Some toxic people like to sign people up to spam. They are being nice and helpful by assuming that we all suffer from erectile dysfunction, want a Russian bride, and are due significant tax rebates.

Spam filters are usually pretty effective, but if you're getting a high number of spam emails, or you're receiving harassing emails, it's worth considering changing your email address. This can be inconvenient, but it's free and easy to do. It could save you a lot of emotional hassle. Just as when changing your number, be cautious about who you give your email address to, and where you share it online.

Crawling out of the woodwork

It's not uncommon for toxic people to show up in your life when you least expect them to. They seem to have a knack for showing up at the worst times.

Toxic people come back into your life for a reason. It's always because they want something. It might be a place to stay, money, or they want to inflict some more pain on you. In any circumstances, it's best to err on the side of caution.

Laura's story
Laura's father had raised her since she was five. Her mother walked out on them, deciding she would rather travel the world as a free woman than be a mother tied to her child.

Although he was devastated, Laura's father did his best to bring her up as a single parent, and he did a great job. He made sure she got a good education – but, most of all, that she felt loved.

As the years passed, Laura slowly forget about her mother. Her mother didn't make contact for sixteen years, and became a distant memory. That was, until Laura's twenty-first birthday, when she received a Facebook message. It was from her mother. It read:

Hi Laura,

I know it's been a long time, but I just wanted to wish you a happy birthday.

I hope you get some nice presents and everything you want.

Sandra (your mum)

Her mum's mobile phone number was underneath.

Laura was shocked. She showed the message to her father, and they looked at each other in bemusement. A whole raft of emotions and thoughts rushed through Laura's mind – anger, excitement, confusion. She didn't know what to make of it.

Her dad suggested she forget about the message for the day, so she could focus on enjoying her birthday with her friends. Laura took her father's advice, and went to the party and meal she had arranged with her friends. But she couldn't stop thinking about her mother's message, and her friends could see there was something on her mind. Rather than enjoy her birthday meal, the same thoughts went round and round inside her head.

'Why has she made contact with me?'
'What is she like?'
'Has she changed?'

Laura met her father the next day, and they chatted about the message. They discussed whether or not it was a good idea for Laura to reply. Laura only had faint memories of her mum and, like any child who hadn't seen their mother for over sixteen years; she was inquisitive and wanted to find out more.

Her father had been married to her mum for over five years. He had vivid memories of the reasons she had walked out all those years ago, so he was naturally a lot more cautious. He was a protective father, and he didn't want his daughter to get hurt again.

After a lengthy debate, Laura's curious nature won, and they agreed she would make contact. Her father wasn't happy about her decision because he didn't trust his ex but, rather than dictate the situation, he decided to help Laura and manage it the best he could. He knew, if she didn't make contact, she would regret it.

That evening, Laura called her mum.

Sandra: Hello.

Laura: Hi. It's me, Laura.

Sandra: Hi, Laura. So you got my message?

Laura: Yes, thanks.

Laura wasn't sure what to say. Her mum was talking to her as though there was nothing wrong – just like she would speak to a friend she had met just yesterday.

Sandra: So, did you have a nice birthday?

Laura began to get agitated. A nice birthday? *she thought.* What about the last sixteen years? *Shocked by her mother's passive attitude, she didn't say what was on her mind, opting to stay silent. The conversation continued awkwardly for a few more minutes. Laura wanted to give her mother a chance, and agreed to speak to her again the next day.*

The second conversation

Sandra: Hello.

Laura: Hi. It's me, Laura.

Sandra: Hi, darling. When are we meeting up?

Laura: I'd rather get to know you a little more first.

Sandra: What do you mean? I'm your mother.

Shocked at her mother's audacity, Laura began to get angry.

Laura: You walked out on us when I was five. You haven't been in touch for sixteen years.

Sandra: I'm in touch now.

At this point, Laura started to regret contacting her mother. The reasons her dad had given, including his concern that her mum might let Laura down and she would get hurt, were becoming a reality. She got upset.

Laura: Why now? Why after sixteen years? Why haven't you been in touch earlier? You left me when I was five. You haven't even said why. You've not apologised once.

Sandra: I told your father why at the time.

Laura: You left me because you wanted to travel the world. Do you know how much that hurts?

Sandra: It felt right at the time.

Laura: And how does it feel now?

Sandra: I was young. It wasn't my fault. I had no choice.

Laura: You always have a choice. You didn't have to leave me and not speak to me for sixteen years!

Sandra: I'm speaking to you now. I'm not perfect, but I'm your mum. You take me as you find me.

Laura: I don't need you. I'm doing better without you.

Sandra: What – you don't need your own mother?

Laura: You haven't been in my life for over sixteen years.

Sandra: If you feel like that, there's nothing I can do about it.

Sandra hung up. Laura was devastated, and lots of emotions and thoughts raced around her mind. Later, she saw her dad and told him about the conversation, sobbing uncontrollably. He hugged her and told her that everything will be OK.

Laura learned a lot from her experience. Let's start from the beginning.

Social media: Social media has made it much easier for people to find people – and for your past to catch up with you. As you just saw, you have to be cautious about what information you share online. The rule goes: if you don't want it to be public, don't share it on social media.

Actions speak louder than words: Laura's mum walked out on her when Laura was five. She did it because she wanted to go and travel the world, leaving her five-year-old child behind. What person with any conscience would do that? Her actions speak much louder than her words.

Dysfunctional behaviour: There was no substance to the first message Laura received. Is that the type of message you would expect from a mother who had walked out on her child sixteen years ago? The telephone conversation started with her mother acting as though nothing untoward had happened. Is that normal behaviour? By the start of the second conversation, Laura's mother was asking to meet her. She didn't allow Laura to get to know her and set the pace, as a rational person would.

No remorse, explanation or apology: Laura's mum didn't see anything as her fault. She did not apologise, explain or show remorse. She wasn't a big enough person to admit she had done wrong. If she was, she probably wouldn't have walked out in the first place.

Leopards don't change their spots: Even after sixteen years, it would be optimistic to think that her mother would have changed for the better – without her mother proving she had changed by apologising and changing her behaviour. Is this unfair? No more unfair than her mother leaving Laura when she was a child. If Laura's mother was capable of leaving her five-year-old daughter, what else is she capable of? If Laura had met her mother as an adult, it would probably only have been a matter of time before her mother created unwanted drama in Laura's life.

Forgive, but don't forget: Laura shouldn't allow anger and resentment to eat her up. She should forgive, and let go – for herself. Forgiving her mother doesn't mean that Laura has to accept her with open arms. Laura's mother might see forgiveness as weakness, but only if Laura allows her to continue treating her badly. If Laura decided to continue talking to or seeing her mother, it would be up to Laura to adopt the techniques she felt most appropriate for the situation. In this instance, when her mother hung up on Laura, based on her history, it would be best for Laura not to have any further contact.

What is the intention?: If Laura's mother showed no remorse, and was unable to demonstrate any type of rational or functional behaviour, what was her intention when she contacted Laura? If it wasn't to be nice and to make amends for the past, what *was* it for? Laura's mother was quick to end the call when she found out that Laura wouldn't be as easy to manipulate as she thought she would be. Is that what she wanted – somebody she could easily manipulate? What type of person wants a relationship with their daughter based on manipulation? Those intentions are cruel, and nobody should have a relationship with anybody who believes they can treat someone in this way.

Using caution
Laura's story teaches us why we need to exert caution with toxic people, no matter who they are.

Sometimes toxic behaviour isn't so obvious and up-front. You should always err on the side of caution, whether you have doubts about someone or not. If you jump in with both feet, you're leaving yourself wide open to getting hurt. Don't jump into something without giving it a little time.

If somebody who has previously demonstrated toxic behaviour comes back into your life, you should judge them on their previous actions. Give them the opportunity to show you what their real intentions are. Eventually, their intentions will always become apparent.

How much time you give them is up to you. It always pays to err on the side of caution, though. If, after a period of time, they've shown they might have changed, it's OK (and natural) to take your guard down a little. Just don't take it down completely, and open yourself up too much. Use your common sense and listen to your gut instinct.

Toxic behaviour doesn't resolve toxic behaviour

Toxic behaviour will never resolve toxic behaviour, just as fire doesn't put out fire. You should never resort to lowering your standards in the hope that, if you go down to a toxic person's level, they might see sense.

The only way to dissolve toxicity is by killing it with kindness. Douse it with love. Cover it with compassion. This is the last thing a toxic person expects. They want you to go down to their level. They want you to get angry, shout, swear and argue. They want to pull you right down with them. It's their sole purpose. Don't let them win.

I know it's incredibly hard, and I have no doubt at times you'll be very tempted to give them a piece of what they are dishing out to you. Who wouldn't? But you have to remember, toxic behaviour will only ever add to toxic behaviour.

It's up to you to be an eagle and soar. Leave the pigeons to act as they please. As a reminder, here are some of the behaviours an eagle would never resort to.

Violence

We've all heard stories about bullying being ended by the victim punching the bully in the nose. Violence isn't the answer when it comes to dealing with toxic people.

No matter how placid you are, a toxic person will sometimes push you to your very limit. They will say terrible things to you on purpose. Do terrible things to you. Your blood will boil. You will feel like you want to do horrible things to them. You might imagine doing these things, and get pleasure from it.

However, stick to imagining these things. Violence is never the answer. Violence can lead to a criminal record, a prison sentence, to situations that you can't turn back from, and that you might regret for the rest of your life. No toxic person is worth that.

Instead of resorting to violence, my advice is to buy a punch bag or some other punching implement (your sofa cushions need a good plump-up every now and again) you can easily, regularly access. Another effective release of anger is exercise. I am a regular at the gym, and it's not always because I want a body like Adonis. I find lifting weights is a good way to release tension. My gym also has a punch bag, which means I don't have to have one at home. I also find high-impact sports, such as squash, great to release tension.

Find things that work for you. If you haven't tried it already, I highly recommend exercise. Not only is it good for getting rid of anger and tension, but it also has endless other benefits for you, your health and your well-being.

Retaliation

When you get a shitty email or text, don't be tempted to send one back. Don't allow your anger and need for retaliation to spoil all your hard work.

I know your finger will hover over the send button, ready to send the message: GO AND FUCK YOURSELF. But you have to remember: toxic people thrive on your attention. It is exactly what they want. He sent you that message to get your reaction. He wants to see that his words have made an impact on you. He wants to see you hurt and angry.

You are an eagle. You don't need to react to pigeons.

Starve him of your attention, no matter how angry and frustrated he has made you. If it helps, rant to a friend about how you're feeling, or go and punch something (a cushion is ideal, and usually in the vicinity). Whatever you do, don't react. Leave your laptop, phone, tablet – whatever it is – and give yourself the time and space you need to breathe, calm down and think rationally. That is how an eagle acts.

Arguing

Mark Twain said that you should never argue with stupid people, because they'll drag you down to their level and then beat you with experience! He wasn't only right about arguing with stupid people – he was right about toxic people, too.

There's no point in arguing. It doesn't get you anywhere, especially with toxic people. Your reason and all your points might heavily outweigh theirs, and after the argument there may be no doubt you're the undisputed winner, but how have you made the other person feel? You'll just make the toxic person angrier at you. And that isn't a win for you.

I know – they deserve to be put in their place. But at what cost? The outcome we're looking for here is one that works for you.

Arguing can quickly become a daily and regular occurrence, especially if the toxic person is somebody you live with and spend lots of time with, such as a partner or child.

Arguing will only continue the dysfunctional cycle. Somebody has to be big enough to put an end to it, otherwise, every time you see that person your brain will revert to the default setting of arguing. And that makes you toxic yourself.

A toxic person will see arguing as everyday normal behaviour, but you shouldn't. Life is miserable when you argue all the time. It's not pleasurable, so you have to be the eagle. You have to stop arguing back. If the toxic person persists (which is likely), don't get sucked in. Use the techniques you've learned in this book, including walking away if necessary.

Getting addicted

A lot of us have addictive tendencies. Some addictions, such as to smoking and alcohol, are obvious – but lots aren't so apparent. We may be harbouring addictions that manifest themselves through toxic behaviour. Let's focus on some obvious addictions, such as overeating.

When we overeat, we're trying to fill a void. The void is usually an emotion, such as love. If you're starved of love, you might find comfort from eating a lot. Look at it like this. If we can fill ourselves up by drinking water, why do we prefer to eat chocolate cake instead? Drinking water doesn't give us that *ummmm*, does it? Water won't make you obese, but chocolate cake will. Obesity is bad for our health, which is why we need to look at filling the void in other ways.

When we smoke a cigarette, it's a comfort thing. When we drink alcohol, it might be a numbing thing. When we take illegal drugs, it's likely to help us escape. Like obesity, all these things can have serious consequences for our health.

It is ultimately up to you if you become addicted to something. But it is worthwhile me pointing out that you may be turning to a crutch because of a toxic person. If you're constantly being hammered down by physical or mental abuse, or you're made to feel unloved or neglected, you might look to fill that void by overeating, drinking, smoking or taking drugs. However, ultimately it is up to you to make sure you deal with the toxicity in your life in a good, effective way, not a self-destructive way.

If you have loving, caring people in your life, you have no void. It doesn't guarantee that you won't be tempted to drink or smoke, but it will certainly decrease the odds of you taking drugs or indulging in some other form of escapism.

If you're a loving person, you deserve to have loving people in your life – much in the same way that, if you're a toxic person, you deserve toxic people in yours. I believe you call it karma...

Involving other people
Don't use other people as pawns, especially children. Dealing with a toxic person – in a relationship, for example – might mean you resorting to pulling out all the stops to resolve an issue. Children tend to be the victims in these circumstances because they can get stuck in the middle of toxic behaviour.

They are the innocent parties. Where possible, shield them from negative behaviour, don't expose them to it. They are like sponges: they're taking in everything that happens to them, and they're learning from their parents how to live their lives as adults, and how to deal with other people. Try to set them a good example.

Remember what I said earlier about toxicity running in families? By putting your kids in the middle, you're teaching them that this is how relationships work. You're vastly increasing the odds that they will act in the same way when they are old enough to have relationships.

No matter how you feel about the other person, don't get into the habit of bad-mouthing them to your children. If you have few people to talk to, your kids can seem like the perfect sounding board for everything that's on your mind. Think twice before you do it. An innocent kid doesn't want to know how useless his dad is, or how much of a bitch his mum is, no matter how true you think it is. You aren't protecting them by telling them what you believe is the truth. All you're doing is affecting them mentally, in a negative way.

Your children are innocent, and they should stay that way. They deserve that opportunity. I'm not saying you have to mollycoddle them; just aim to get the balance right. Teach them the ways of the world, but don't destroy it before they get a chance to see it for themselves and make their own minds up.

If your children aren't old enough to protect themselves from toxicity, it's your job as a parent to protect them – especially if they are too young to communicate how they feel. At the same time (and this is where the balance comes in to play), don't be too possessive of them. Let them learn and grow. As they grow up, they'll make their own mistakes – that's the only way they'll learn for themselves.

Settling for less

We've covered lots of reasons why staying in a toxic environment is bad for you, and why you deserve more than to settle for second best.

Don't stay in the hope that their toxic behaviour will eventually change. Don't wait for them to eventually like you. Don't try to win their affection or love. If they're not giving you what you're giving them, you deserve more.

Staying will only cause you more heartache and pain. If a relationship (of any kind) is over, deep down you'll know that it's time to let go and move on. If it's allowed to go on, it could lead to you demonstrating the type of toxic behaviour you've been learning to avoid in this book, including jealousy and obsession.

If you are struggling to let go of a relationship, go and talk to somebody straightaway. Speak to a friend, an experienced counsellor, or somebody impartial such as a support worker at an organisation, and tell them how you feel. It will help you work through what's on your mind, so you can move forward in a positive way.

Revenge

As I said earlier in the book, it takes a strong person to get hurt and not want to hurt other people in revenge. Toxic people will want to get revenge because they cannot stand the thought of somebody getting one up on them. This type of mentality is built on insecurity and feelings of inadequacy.

Would a happy and secure person want to get revenge, or would they view every situation as a learning curve and move on? Only unhappy, insecure, toxic people seek revenge. You have to decide who you want to be.

Sticking up for yourself and defending your welfare are very different to getting revenge. Cutting somebody out of your life because they have treated you poorly is not revenge. The toxic person might view it this way. They might see it as you punishing them. When you don't think anything is your own fault, and take zero responsibility for your actions, that's how you're going to view it.

Frank Sinatra once said 'the best revenge is massive success'. You're an eagle. You're big enough to take responsibility for your actions. You are happy and secure. You don't need to get revenge. You just need to go out and live your life – and find the 'massive success' you deserve.

Moving on from toxic behaviour

Moving on from toxic behaviour is a big decision, especially if there are other factors at play – and there usually are. Like all big decisions, it should be well thought out. If it isn't, it's likely to lead to further problems in the future. If you regret your decision and move on, but then decide to give the toxic person another chance, you might find yourself in a constant cycle of going back and forth.

If you feel you've done everything you can, and the relationship has gone past the point of reconciliation – if your common sense and instinct are telling you that things will never change – you need to be able to move on.

As I said at the start of this book, dealing with toxic behaviour is never easy. But you have to be honest – not only with yourself, but also with the people who are demonstrating toxic behaviour. You should always communicate how you feel, whether or not you think they are listening. When you reach the point where you believe communication is no longer working – if you feel as though you are flogging a dead horse – it's time to move on and expect change.

If you decide to move on, try not to leave any grey areas. We all need closure. Leaving things open to interpretation by not communicating will only lead to future problems.

Even if they haven't shown you respect and treated you well, it doesn't mean you have to act in the same way. You may want to immediately close off all communication. In cases of abuse, having no further contact is understandable, but in most circumstances you should never close the door without being completely straight and honest. This can lead to the problems we covered earlier. That also means being brave. Ending a relationship by text, for example, only shows your weakness. How would you feel if somebody did that to you?

You have several options, and I've listed them here. In all these circumstances, as you learned in the last chapter, the aim is to be the bigger person – the eagle. If you feel you're being sucked into the toxic behaviour, end the communication. At that point you know you have tried everything you can, and your conscience should be clear.

All these examples rely on your common sense. If you've been the victim of physical abuse, for example, meeting face-to-face could put you in more danger. In this instance, the other options are more appropriate.

A telephone conversation may be the best way for you to express how you feel, and give you the opportunity to tell them why you've reached your decision.

All the options will come with a level of discomfort, and ultimately, you must choose the option you feel most comfortable with. If you choose not to communicate, in the hope that things will magically resolve themselves, it needs to be with the understanding that they rarely do.

Have a telephone conversation
In a calm manner, tell them why you feel the way you do and why you feel it's best that you no longer see each other.

It's natural to be nervous, and it's OK to express emotion. But it's important for you to put your points across in a confident manner. If it makes you feel more prepared, write down your reasons and what you want to say in the call to refer to if you need to. Focus on your breathing and keep your voice low and slow.

You might find they react with disbelief or anger. If you find resistance to your decision, reiterate your reasons. If they become abusive or derogatory, don't be afraid to end the conversation.

Meet in person

As I mentioned above, sometimes meeting in person isn't the best option. But if you feel confident you can have a face-to-face conversation without physical abuse, meeting in person is the most honourable and brave way to communicate.

Pick somewhere quiet – a place where you can talk. If you feel safer, pick a public place. Deliver your message in a confident manner, and repeat your points if you need to.

If at any point you don't feel safe, don't be afraid to leave.

Write a letter/email

If you're not the best communicator, and you don't feel confident, you also have the option of writing down how you feel.

This may provide relief for you, but it's also an effective way of getting everything off your chest. It gives the person you send it to an opportunity to read it more than once, which might help them appreciate why you feel the way you do.

The one important caveat I would like to add here is that an email can come across as impersonal as a text message, therefore it can appear as though you are 'chickening out'. The same goes for a message being sent over social media.

These types of communication can be looked upon as you not caring. That's why you might also want to consider a handwritten letter. It shows that you have taken time to put it together, and is more likely to deliver your message in an effective way.

Use a third party
Like using text messages and emails, using a third party can make you appear weak, unless there is a valid reason for doing it.

You're an adult, and gone are the days of getting your mum to call in sick for you. On most occasions, taking responsibility and dealing with things yourself is the best policy.

The only valid reason for getting a third party involved is if you feel your well-being or welfare might be compromised.

It might fuel the situation if you get your dad to go and 'sort out' the boyfriend who won't leave you alone, so you need to use your common sense. If things have escalated beyond your control, you should always contact the police. If children are involved, for example, they can act as mediators, and can provide a safe environment for all parties.

Always remember what you learned in the last chapter. Toxic behaviour doesn't resolve toxic behaviour. Always be the bigger person – always be the eagle.

Reopening contact

You may change your mind in future and decide that you want to reopen contact with the toxic person. If you weren't able to resolve all your issues at the time, you may feel that you need closure.

You might feel as though you have unfinished business, or a personal connection, and you might be intrigued enough to pick up the phone, write a letter, or make contact in another way.

If you decide to do that, do it with an open mind. Don't go in with any expectations. The toxic person may have decided to re-educate themselves, and therefore they are more able to have a healthy relationship with you. Or their behaviour could have become worse. You have to be open to, and comfortable with, all possible scenarios.

The most important thing is that you are moving forward on your journey. Don't try to force anything, and do what is right for you. If a person is meant to be part of your journey, they will be.

Moving forward on your journey

In the book, I've mentioned the past wanting to drag you back in, and how easy it is to allow this to happen. I want to end the book by reiterating the importance of moving forward.

I want your change to last – to be for life – and I don't want all your hard work to be for nothing. That means you having forward momentum, and being comfortable with change. It's natural to feel guilty and experience other negative emotions when you leave the past behind but, if you want good things to happen to you, you have to keep moving forward on your journey.

And life is a journey – don't forget that.

This journey, like any journey worth taking, will consist of ups and downs. You will face challenges, including toxic behaviour. You just have to remember to maintain your forward momentum, and not allow negative people and situation to hold you back or stand in your way.

You should always have something to move forward *for*. Your health, and knowing you have no regrets, should be all the motivation you need.

Your health, happiness and well-being

There is nothing more important than how you feel. If toxic people are constantly dragging you down, your well-being – along with everything else positive in your life – will take a serious hit.

When it comes to your health, there's no messing about. What do you have without your health – both physical and mental? I mention mental health here because it's too easy to dismiss it. When we are physically ill, it is obvious. When we are mentally ill, it's not always obvious until it's too late. That's when conditions such as anxiety and depression can take over and, before you know it, you become consumed by them.

You should always remember that your physical and mental health are entwined. How you feel on the inside will directly affect your physical state. In other words, if you keep allowing toxic people to affect you and your life, you run the risk of getting mentally *and* physically ill. This should be enough for anybody to take action and stay aware because, as I said above, what do you have if you don't have your health?

No regrets

This is a cliché, I know, but it's essential to realise and appreciate that life is short. You only have one life, and if you don't make the most of it, you'll regret it.

The existence of an afterlife has not been proven, and I'm not sure it ever will be. So we need to value the life we've been given. On average, we have about eighty years to live. Time passes quickly.

As Lucille Ball said, 'I'd rather regret the things I have done than the things that I haven't.' Don't spend your life regretting not doing more with your life, or regretting that you wasted it allowing toxic people to make you unhappy.

Putting value on your life means not accepting anything less than you deserve. It means living by your standards, and not compromising.

Whether or not you get more or less than eighty years, life is short. Remembering that you're going to die might be the wake-up call you need.

Seeing people die around me – especially people wh are younger than me – has woken me up. I hope tha this book has acted as your wake-up call, and told yo that you don't have to do something if you don't wan to do it. You don't have to allow toxic people into your life if you don't want to. It's up to you to decide on your future, not anybody else. Choose wisely, and make every day count.

I want to end the book on a positive note by reminding you what I've been telling you from the very beginning:

You are special.

You are unique.

You are loved.

You *can* change.

Nobody can ever take any of these things away from you.

o

u

Summary

It's important for you to remember what I said at the start of the book. As well as toxic people, there are lots of amazing people out there – people who are right for you and will be good for you and your life. When you go out with a positive and optimistic outlook, you'll attract the same type of person, so you'll be a lot less worried about who is toxic and who isn't.

As you progress on your journey of detoxification, toxic people will try and draw you back in. It's up to you if you allow that to happen. It's also up to you whether or not you choose to be a victim. It is a choice – it's *your* choice – so continue to make the right one.

Whatever decision you make from now on, including which techniques you use (or don't use), remember that communication is key. Many relationships break down because of a lack of communication. Things will change only if we communicate what is on our minds, rather than expecting everybody else to be telepathic. Don't forget to communicate with others – and with yourself. Regularly ask yourself how you're feeling, and don't bottle things up inside.

Whenever you might be feeling stuck or alone, remember there are lots of people out there who can help you. You are never alone. Never be ashamed to ask for help.

Facing up to toxic people, whoever they are, will never be easy. But I can guarantee you that it's not as hard as putting up with toxic behaviour for the rest of your life.

Quite simply, you deserve more. Life is too short to put up with anything less than the respect you deserve. Embrace the amazing people in your life, and continue to serve notice on those who no longer adhere to the rules and standards you have set to maintain your well-being and welfare, including your physical and mental health.

You are unique, and that makes you special. You're an eagle, so go and soar like one. Don't allow anybody to convince you of anything else. Their opinion does not count. What *you* believe is the only thing that matters.

If people continue to challenge these facts, rules and standards, tell them to *expect change*.

Continue your journey...

Find more details on my website:

www.carlvernon.com

Sign up to my updates, check out my podcast and blog, take one of my courses, or drop me a line on social media.

Here's to positive change. Cheers!

Take care and best wishes,

Carl Vernon

Printed in Great Britain